DEMONSTRATIONS AND EXPERIMENTS IN SCIENCE

Dr Ben Crystall

Croner Publications Ltd
Croner House
London Road
Kingston upon Thames
Surrey KT2 6SR
Telephone: 0181-547 3333.

Copyright © 1997 Croner Publications Ltd

Published by
Croner Publications Ltd
Croner House
London Road
Kingston upon Thames
Surrey KT2 6SR
Telephone: 0181-547 3333

All rights reserved.
No part of this publication may be reproduced,
stored in a retrieval system, or transmitted in any form or by
any means, electronic, mechanical, photocopying, recording
or otherwise, without the prior permission of
Croner Publications Ltd.

While every care has been taken
in the writing and editing of this book,
readers should be aware that only Acts of Parliament
and Statutory Instruments have the force of law,
and that only the courts can authoritatively
interpret the law.

British Library Cataloguing-in-Publication Data.
A catalogue record for this book
is available from the British Library.

ISBN 1 85524 401 2

Printed by Whitstable Litho Printers Ltd, Whitstable, Kent

THE AUTHOR

DR BEN CRYSTALL is a full-time science writer based in London, currently writing for the *New Scientist*. He spent eight years as a research fellow in the Department of Chemistry at Imperial College, London. Ben is still involved in the Imperial College Schools Lecture Series, during which he has lectured to teachers and students both in the UK and Malaysia.

Ben has written numerous papers and articles for a variety of publications and has been awarded a Royal Society/Committee for the Public Understanding of Science grant to promote the public understanding of science.

THE REVIEWERS

ILYA EIGENBROT currently works at Imperial College and at the Royal Institution of Great Britain in London. He has been involved in the development of a wide range of demonstration lectures for many years, and worked on the BBC Christmas Lecture Series in 1996.

Ilya has lectured both in this country and abroad, and is a firm believer in the importance of demonstrations for the effective teaching of science. He has received several Royal Society/Committee for the Public Understanding of Science grants to promote the public understanding of science.

STEPHEN DENGATE has taught science in a range of secondary schools and was a Head of Science. He became an advisory teacher before developing his career as a LEA inspector/adviser. He is now the County Consultant for Science for Surrey LEA and a manager in their advisory and inspection service, the Curriculum & Management Consultancy.

Stephen is an OFSTED inspector and provider of in-service training in all phases of education. He is an experienced science adviser, one of the main contributors to Croner's *Manual for Heads of Science* and editorial co-ordinator for the *Heads of Science Briefing*.

Do You Require Additional Copies of This Book?

Additional copies are available at a special price of £9.95, including postage and packing, and can be ordered by telephoning our Customer Services team on 0181-547 3333. Please quote ref KRRT.

CONTENTS

THE ROLE OF DEMONSTRATIONS AND EXPERIMENTS
What Are Demonstrations And Experiments?	2
Why Carry Them Out?	3
What They Should Offer	4

LIGHT AND COLOUR
White Light	7
Using Light For Analysis	16
Polarised Light	32
Reactions Observed by Colour Change	38
Lasers and Laser Experiments	51

MATERIALS AND PHYSICAL PROCESSES
Polymers	65
Non-Newtonian Liquids	72
Other Demonstrations	79

LIFE PROCESSES
DNA	85
Plants and their Properties	89
Osmosis	93
Capillary Action	96
Other Processes	98

COMPUTERS AND THE INTERNET
Build Your Own Displays	105
Information via the Internet	106

SAFETY ISSUES
Laser Safety	111
Useful Publications	113

FURTHER INFORMATION
- Science Questions — 115
- Drama and Exhibitions — 116
- Universities and Colleges — 116
- Useful Publications — 117
- Suppliers — 119

INDEX

INTRODUCTION

The use of science demonstrations and experiments as methods for teaching is long established, but as the breadth and depth of available knowledge has increased and the requirements of the curriculum have been expanded teachers have often found themselves being forced to rely increasingly on the use of text-based rather than activity-based teaching. However, learning through experimentation is still a vital and important part of the science curriculum and almost all science teachers will expend great amounts of time and effort preparing and developing demonstrations and experiments for the classroom. Most surprisingly, this is an area for which very little formal training is available. This book aims to provide teachers with useful background material, experimental suggestions and resource listings.

The majority of demonstrations and experiments in this book can be performed by teachers (and many by pupils themselves) with minimal modifications to suit specific needs. They illustrate the range of styles that can be used and subjects that can be covered. They can also be used as the basis for developing further demonstrations and experiments. The descriptions that follow include a discussion of what the demonstrations and experiments should show and how they attempt to illustrate it. Other important considerations include knowing how and why they work as they do and also, in some cases, what could go wrong and why.

The chemical demonstrations and experiments include recipes for making the compounds and information on their use and disposal. Some of the demonstrations and experiments involve the use of hazardous materials. Although some safety guidance is given it should by no means be seen as comprehensive. Further information on the hazards, storage and use of chemicals can be found in Croner's *Manual for Heads of Science*.

All teachers should carry out their own careful safety assessment of any chemicals and equipment used in demonstrations and experiments for the first time. The publishers cannot accept responsibility for any accidents arising from the demonstrations and experiments detailed in this book. Pupil safety is the responsibility of the teacher carrying out the activity.

CHAPTER 1

THE ROLE OF DEMONSTRATIONS AND EXPERIMENTS

"Wonderful are the capacities of experiments to lead us into various departments of knowledge."

Michael Faraday

The origins of using demonstrations and experiments to accompany scientific teaching go back a long way. Before the widespread availability of textbooks and other sources of printed information one of the main methods of teaching was to demonstrate techniques and subjects directly to pupils. Scientific demonstrations formed an important part of teaching up until the 1930s. Since World War Two this situation has changed considerably as the breadth of subjects studied in schools has increased and the preparation time available to teachers has decreased. However, in recent years efforts have been made to reintroduce demonstration lecturing into science education as part of the attempt to reverse the current trend of fewer pupils opting for the sciences.

Many would describe the Royal Institution in London as the home of the scientific demonstration, due to its long association with the Friday Evening Discourse and with promoting what is now called the public understanding of science. It also holds a series of televised Christmas lectures for young people which are almost theatrical in style.

Demonstrations and Experiments in Science

Drama has an important role to play in scientific education. Increasing numbers of scientists are using demonstrations, comedy and other activities in an attempt to capture the interest of young people. These include many institutions and groups, such as the Science Museum and the Floating Point Theatre Company. Together with the assistance of funding bodies such as the Royal Society and the growing publicity surrounding events such as National Science Week, this expansion in activity serves to illustrate the increasing emphasis on portraying science to all audiences in an eye-catching, imaginative way.

WHAT ARE DEMONSTRATIONS AND EXPERIMENTS?

Demonstrations and experiments can only be defined fairly loosely as the boundary between what constitutes an experiment and a demonstration is blurred. For the purpose of this book, the terms demonstration and experiment are used interchangeably. An experiment is traditionally viewed as where pupils are involved in performing an activity or technique which illustrates a message, law or series of points. A demonstration is what the teacher does to display the experiment to pupils.

In contrast to purely text-based learning, demonstrations and experiments provide an extra degree of activity or participation for both teacher and pupil. Although the use of demonstrations and experiments can cause problems where timetabling is already tight and since, in most cases, teachers have heavy workloads, they can also be very rewarding.

Some scientists and teachers argue that 'lecture experiments' lose their effectiveness if they become 'lecture demonstrations', since once they lose their experimental nature they inherently fail to represent scientific method. This is a problem which can only be overcome through the method of presentation. A demonstration can be presented as an experiment and still fail. Demonstrations can teach students much about experimental science. It should be stressed that demonstrations and experiments should not be formal events, rather they should act to stimulate discussion and questions.

WHY CARRY THEM OUT?

Demonstrations and experiments have an important role to play in science education. They have a number of features which can complement other forms of teaching.

1. They can provide a dramatic element and have a visual impact which can be both memorable and enjoyable for pupils and teachers.
2. They are events which provide a class with an opportunity to break from the routine of text-based learning.
3. They also provide an opportunity for teaching details of experimental technique, such as those related to laboratory safety, the safe handling of chemicals and dangerous equipment, and the proper use of protective clothing.

Taken together, the factors listed above should motivate pupils and give them a chance to see science not merely as a series of laws and equations to be memorised but as an active area of enquiry.

Demonstrations need not be performed solely by the teacher. Some may only be performed once due to the requirements for complex or delicate equipment, or simply due to limitations of time or cost. By allowing pupils to participate directly in experiments, teachers can communicate what the process of science is actually all about: asking questions, making observations based on the results of experiments and developing trains of thought to account for these results. Pupils may then be able to suggest further experiments which might be able to confirm their observations.

The role of demonstrations and experiments is to facilitate the learning of facts directly by observation and participation. Often, in order to make science interesting and memorable, we need to provide a vivid mental image. The science that we remember in later life is frequently that which we found stimulating and exciting at the time.

WHAT THEY SHOULD OFFER

Good science demonstrations and experiments have a number of essential characteristics. Most importantly, they should be appropriate to the subject area being covered in class at the time and carry a point or message which should reinforce other class work. They should be visible to all the students, impressive and, within reason, on as large a scale as possible. Many of the best demonstrations and experiments are simple and, of course, all must be safe for both demonstrator and audience. They should involve audience participation if possible and always be well practised and rehearsed so that the above aims can be achieved. However, even when they go wrong (and they will) demonstrations and experiments are still useful, for example through the questions they pose. Why have they failed? How could they be improved? These problems are all part of the scientific process; to most research scientists, a failed experiment is more common than a successful one. An error designed into a demonstration or experiment can be a good test of observation and knowledge.

Demonstrations and experiments can be used within the boundaries of the National Curriculum to develop pupils' experimental and investigative skills. This involves training pupils to make predictions, to take careful consideration of variables and to be able to record evidence and results clearly. They should gain experience in analysing and explaining results, including explanations of how and why an experiment went wrong. Pupils should also be able to suggest improvements to an experiment, appreciating its limitations, its reliability and the potential errors implicit in its design. Experiments will give pupils an opportunity to use a range of apparatus which they may not otherwise encounter and will give them experience of taking the safety considerations of experiments into account.

The demonstrator should have suitable protective clothing, particularly for some of the demonstrations involving the use of chemicals, and if in any doubt, potentially hazardous demonstrations should be conducted behind a safety screen. Demonstrations can be scaled according to the size of the audience. When scaling chemistry experiments up care should be taken since rates of reaction can change greatly. Demonstrations and experiments should always be practised beforehand so that the teacher can become familiar with their behaviour.

CHAPTER 2

LIGHT AND COLOUR

This chapter looks at light and colour. It deals with the properties of white light, and illustrates light scattering, polarisation and the role of colour change. The final section deals with lasers and their uses in teaching.

WHITE LIGHT

White light from a torch or from an overhead projector is actually made up of many different colours. Our eyes and brain have evolved so as to 'see' this combination of colours as 'white' but there are a number of easy ways in which we can clearly demonstrate the coloured constituents of white light. Sir Isaac Newton was the first person to study the splitting of white light, by a prism and by water, in a systematic way in the seventeenth century.

Why does it happen? Light is an electromagnetic wave. When it enters a material such as a glass prism it is slowed down relative to its speed in a vacuum. This is caused by the positive or negative electrical charges in the solid material delaying the light wave by interacting with the electrical and magnetic fields of the light beam. The different colours in white light are not affected to the same extent. The higher the frequency of the light wave, the more it is slowed by the charges in the material. High frequency, short wavelength violet or blue light is slowed more than the shorter frequency, longer wavelength red light. In other words, the refractive index of glass depends on the colour of the light passing through it.

If light enters a prism at an angle, since blue light slows down more than red light, the light beam will be bent (refracted) and the different colours will follow different paths through the glass prism. As they leave the prism they are dispersed such that a white light spectrum can be seen on a screen. This forms one of the simplest but also one of the most important optical demonstrations. The demonstration requires only simple apparatus, as detailed below.

Equipment required

A slide projector with a bright bulb of at least 100W

A slide made from black card with a narrow (3–4mm) slit cut vertically in the middle

A large glass or plastic prism

A screen or piece of white card

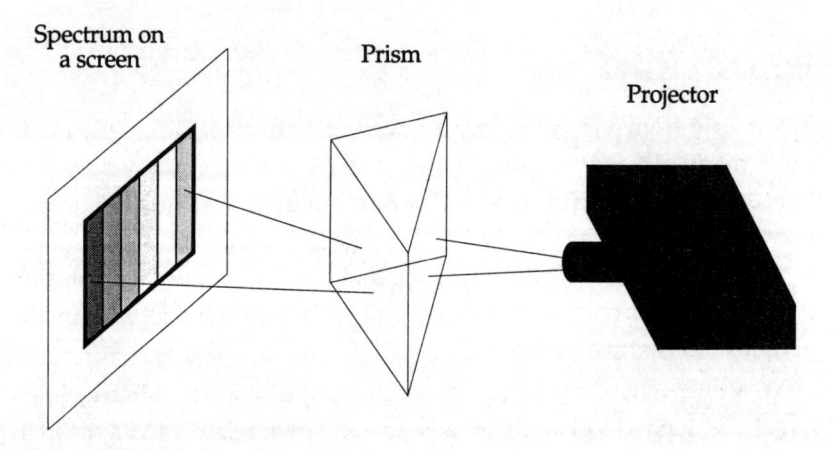

Figure 1

The slide is placed in the projector. The projector is then arranged to shine through one side of the prism. With the correct alignment, the light leaving the prism is split up and a rainbow of colours can be seen on the screen (see figure 1 above).

Light and Colour

An alternative method is to use an overhead projector onto which is placed a piece of cardboard with a cut-out slit about 5mm wide and 10cm long. This provides a narrow source of light which can be used with a prism to produce a large rainbow on a light coloured wall or ceiling. Suitable prisms can be purchased from many sources, for example Philip Harris or Edmund Scientific (see page 119 for contact details), and are relatively cheap.

This demonstration can also be used to show the effect of coloured filters on the transmission of light. By placing red or green filters in front of the projector changes in the spectrum of transmitted light can be seen and certain colours (depending on the filters used) will be absent from the spectrum. These spectra can also be compared with the light produced when shining a red laser through a prism and onto a screen. A single red spot will be visible, showing the colour purity of laser light. It can be shown that even a second prism will not split primary colours (red, green and blue) down any further.

These demonstrations could also form the basis of a series of experiments explaining primary colours. With coloured Wratten gel filters, red, green and blue light can be made to recombine to form an approximation of white light. This demonstration can be carried out using slide projectors as light sources. Three projectors with bulbs of equal wattage should be arranged so that their output images overlap on a white screen. Red, green and blue filters are put into the projectors and primary and secondary colours should become visible. Combining any two primary colours will reveal the secondary colours (cyan, yellow and magenta). Where all three colours overlap, the screen should appear white.

Colour televisions use the three primary colours to produce a full range of colours. Phosphor strips of the primary colours are placed so close together on the screen of the television's picture tube that the eye cannot distinguish between them. If all three adjacent colours are lit up, the screen gives off white light, and by controlling their intensities any mixture of colours can be made to appear.

Simple Wave Experiments

Sound and light travel as waves which have troughs and crests. Sound is a disturbance of air where the wave particles oscillate in the same direction as the wave movement (longitudinal waves), whereas light waves oscillate at right angles to the direction of travel (transverse waves). Both types of wave travel in straight lines unless they meet an obstacle. The purpose of the demonstrations below is to give pupils a basic understanding of the physical properties of waves and the meaning of the terms 'crest' and 'trough'.

Demonstration 1

Equipment required
A metal coil or 'slinky'

The metal coil or 'slinky' is an ideal piece of equipment for demonstrating both longitudinal and transverse waves. One end should be held firmly by a pupil or fixed in position on a bench. The other end should be moved so that the metal coil is extended to a metre or more in length. To demonstrate transverse waves, such as light, the end should be moved sharply upwards and a wave will move along the coil. To show a longitudinal wave, such as sound, the end of the slinky is moved sharply towards the other, fixed end and a wave of compression, followed by rarefaction, will travel down the coil.

Demonstration 2

Equipment required
2 radios

Tune in two radios to the same station and place them about 50cm apart. Have pupils walk quietly about the room listening for dead spots (troughs) and loud spots (crests). Pupils could be told to raise a hand when they enter a trough.

Demonstration 3

Equipment required
A xylophone
5–6 test tubes mounted in a rack (or jars, beakers, etc)
Rubber bands
Empty containers (boxes, plastic cups, lids, etc)

Listen to different pitches on a xylophone. Ask pupils what they think causes the different sounds. They should be allowed to try using the xylophone and then to make their own. A simple home-made xylophone is easily built by pouring different levels of water into test tubes in a rack, or into identical jars, beakers, etc. After trying both the ready-made and the home-made versions, pupils should be able to appreciate that the length of bar or height of water can regulate the pitch of sound waves.

Alternatively, rubber bands of various thicknesses can be stretched across boxes or any small, empty containers to see if they can make graduated sounds, as in a xylophone. The tighter a band is stretched, the faster it vibrates and the higher the pitch of the sound produced.

Demonstration 4

Equipment required
Two strips of masking or strapping tape (3-4 metres long)
A glass pie pan
2–3 drops of food colouring
An overhead projector
2 rods or pencils
80–100 plastic straws (long straws or wooden dowling works best)

This demonstration can be used to illustrate crests and troughs in transverse waves. A glass pie pan is mounted on an overhead projector and filled with water slightly coloured with a food colouring. Waves can be demonstrated by touching a rod or pencil on the surface of the water in the centre of the pan and watching the waves (troughs and crests) move to the edge of the pan and back. Try using two rods or pencils to see what happens when the waves meet. Pupils can also try this for themselves.

Wave machines can be made by groups of pupils to demonstrate the above experiment. The first strip of tape is laid on a table, sticky side up. A pupil should hold each end securely. Others in the class should place straws at half inch intervals along the tape perpendicular to the middle of it. When all the straws have been laid out, the second strip of tape is placed on top of the straws (sticky side down) and above the first strip of tape. The finished product will resemble a spine (tape) and ribs (straws). A pupil should hold each tape end horizontally while a third pushes down on one end, sending a wave pattern from one end of the tape to the other.

From a Prism to a Rainbow

Why can we see a rainbow (coloured spectrum) during a rain shower? If we think of the shape of a glass prism and compare it to a large glass lens, we can see that we may expect the edge of a large lens to also split light into its spectrum, which indeed happens. If we then consider that a glass hemisphere can be created from two fat plano-convex lenses stuck together then we would also expect that a full glass sphere will produce a rainbow. This is shown in figure 2 below.

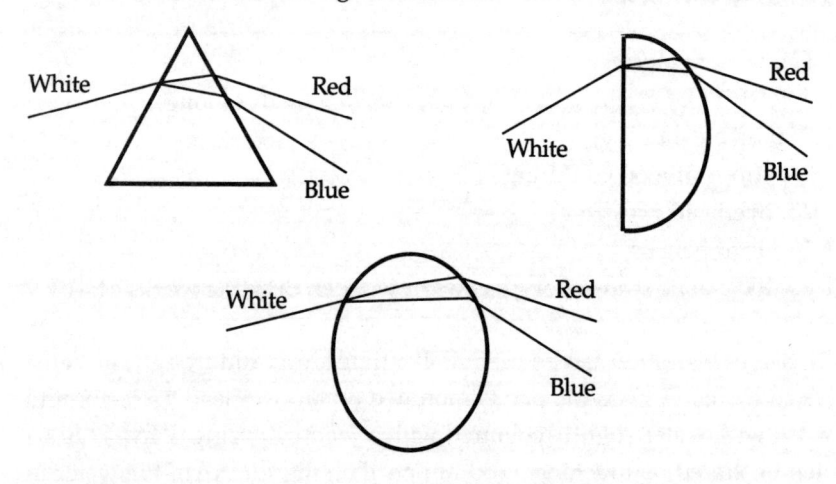

Figure 2

This effect may be shown simply with a large round-bottomed flask full of water and a bright point source of light, such as a slide projector with a pinhole or slit slide. A rainbow is produced by the light shining through the flask of water. Sir Isaac Newton carried out this experiment over 300 years ago using the sun. Sunlight which entered his laboratory through a tiny hole in a curtain acted as a point light source.

Extrapolating from the large round-bottomed flask full of water to smaller and smaller spheres, we can provide an explanation of how it is possible to produce a rainbow from a shower of tiny water droplets. Each water droplet is acting as one tiny prism and hence a rainstorm and sunshine will produce a clearly visible rainbow. This can be simply demonstrated outside using a hosepipe on a sunny day. Putting your thumb over the end of the hosepipe creates a fine mist, and if you have your back to the sun you should be able to see a rainbow.

In some cases, it will be possible to see that a rainbow actually consists of two separate rainbows, one above the other. These are called the primary and secondary rainbows. The first (primary) rainbow is caused by the dispersed light undergoing a single reflection in each water drop and the secondary rainbow is produced as a result of the dispersed light undergoing two reflections. In the case of the primary rainbow, red light is seen at an angle of 42° to the line of the horizon and blue light comes out at about 40°. In the case of the secondary rainbow, which is weaker than the primary, the red light comes out at an angle of 50° to the horizon and blue light comes out at about 54°.

The dispersion of white light by water droplets can also be shown as follows.

Equipment required
A sheet of glass about 15cm square
5-10ml of turpentine
An atomiser

Coat a sheet of glass with soot from burning turpentine in a fume cupboard. Spray the surface with water droplets from an atomiser (available from make-up suppliers) and illuminate the surface with a strong parallel beam of light. Drops of about 0.5mm in diameter will work best. They should be allowed to fall from the atomiser onto the plate perpendicularly, because otherwise they will simply bounce off. The water droplets do not wet the plate: hence they remain almost spherical due to surface tension. When they are viewed from an angle of about 42°, the droplets glisten like individual coloured jewels. This is the result of a single reflection of light within the drops.

Diffraction Gratings

For hundreds of years scientists have used glass prisms to split light into its constituent colours, but more recently it was discovered that any periodic array will also cause splitting of white light to varying degrees. This effect is a result of the diffraction that occurs around the edges of each element of the periodic array. The diffracted light interferes and constructive and destructive interference occurs, with the result that light of different wavelengths is diffracted at different angles and the spectrum of white light is produced.

In fact, the shiny side (the side without labels or writing) of a compact disc will split up white light if it is tilted at the right angle in front of the eye and held towards a bright white light source. The regularly spaced rings of depressions or pits on its surface act as a diffraction grating. In the same way, a vinyl record, when viewed from the right angle and held towards a bright white light, will also disperse white light and produce a spectrum. Any periodic structure on a shiny surface will show this effect. It is also possible to see, although not so clearly, that the millimetre rulings on a metal ruler will generate a spectrum. This is shown in figure 3 opposite.

Light and Colour

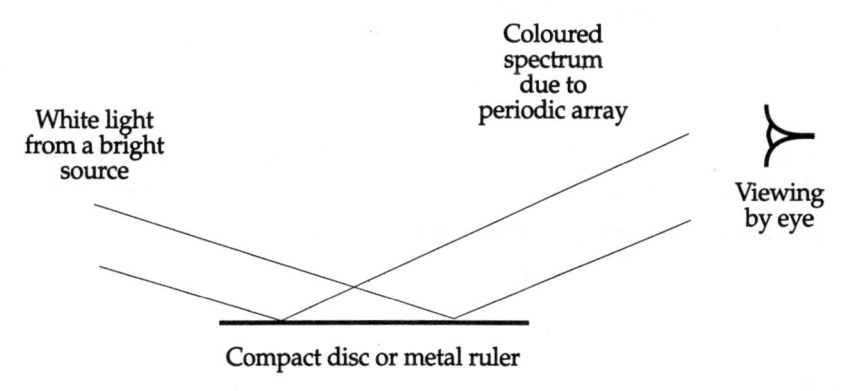

Figure 3

Diagram labels: White light from a bright source; Coloured spectrum due to periodic array; Viewing by eye; Compact disc or metal ruler.

Equipment required
A compact disc, vinyl record or metal ruler
A bright white light source
A SLR camera
A colour camera film
A tripod

The spectra generated by the periodic structure of a compact disc, the grooves of a vinyl record or the millimetre scale on a metal ruler can all be recorded photographically. A bright white light source (100W bulb or more) is best for these experiments and will produce the clearest spectra. An SLR camera should be used for best results. It should be loaded with a fast colour film (ISO 400 or 800). The widest aperture will need to be used for recording spectra from rulers and vinyl records as the spectra are not very bright. A tripod is essential for fixing the camera in place since the exposure times will be very long. Compact discs, however, produce very clear and bright spectra.

USING LIGHT FOR ANALYSIS

There are many different sources of light: light bulbs and fluorescent tubes in the home, neon lights in advertisements and sodium and mercury lights for street lighting. These all convert electrical energy into light energy, but each light source differs in the precise way that it works and the colour of the light that it produces.

Types of Lighting

Light bulbs

An ordinary light bulb uses a thin, double spiral coil of tungsten (the filament). This is mounted in a vacuum or in a low pressure inert gas atmosphere. As an electric current passes through the filament, the electric charges collide with the tungsten atoms and transfer some of their energy to the metal atoms. This electrical heating raises the filament's temperature to about 2500°C and it becomes incandescent. It gives out light of many different wavelengths, some of which we can't see, such as infrared light. In fact, about 85% of the energy from a light bulb is given out as infrared light or heat. The rest of the light mixture appears white to our eyes and it is this small percentage of the total energy given out which we use to light our rooms. The exact shape and 'colour content' of the light bulb's spectrum is dependent on the temperature of the filament. Colour and temperature can be related by Planck's black body radiation equation.

Fluorescent tubes

Fluorescent tubes are more efficient than ordinary light bulbs and give out a different light spectrum. This is due to the materials from which they are made and the way in which they work. A fluorescent light consists of a glass tube filled with mercury vapour which has an electrode at each end. Switching on the electricity supply passes an electrical current through the tube which excites the atoms of mercury which are present in the tube. These excited mercury atoms give off ultraviolet light,

Light and Colour

which is no good on its own for lighting homes because it is invisible to the eye. However, the inside of the glass tube is coated in a phosphor.

Phosphors are mixtures of crystals such as calcium silicate, strontium magnesium phosphate, calcium strontium phosphate and impurities such as manganese and antimony. When a phosphor is illuminated by ultraviolet light it absorbs the light and then re-emits it in a different form as visible light. This visible light energy has slightly less energy than the ultraviolet light that generated it so the extra energy is converted in the phosphor to heat. This causes the fluorescent tubes to warm up after a few minutes. By selecting the exact composition of the phosphor, the manufacturer can tailor the colour of the light emitted by the tube to produce either 'cold' white light or a 'warmer' yellow light.

What these different types of fluorescent tube are actually doing is giving off light with a slightly different light spectrum. Another type of fluorescent tube is called a 'black light'. This looks like a standard fluorescent light but the tube is black and the light given off is almost all ultraviolet light at wavelengths between 300–400nm, with very little in the visible region between 400–600nm. As a result, it appears to give off 'black' light. This ultraviolet light will become visible when it falls on fluorescent paints, or white materials such as T-shirts and white paper which contain artifical brighteners. These are made to glow purple-blue by the ultraviolet light. Teeth are naturally fluorescent and will appear green under ultraviolet light. For this reason black lights are very effective for demonstrations which use fluorescent dyes or paints. The light spectrum given off by a black light is very different to that of a standard fluorescent tube.

Mercury lights

Another light source used at some arenas and football stadiums is the high intensity mercury lamp, which produces a distinctive blue-white light. High pressure metal halide lights are also used outside at these sorts of locations. These lamps also produce a broad range of colours.

Demonstrations and Experiments in Science

Neon and sodium lights

Neon tubes and sodium lamps (called discharge lamps) give off light of very specific colours. This is due to the way in which the light is created: the electrons which orbit around the nucleii of all atoms can exist in different atomic orbitals and each of these corresponds to a particular energy level. By putting energy, in the form of heat or light, into an atom the electrons in the outermost occupied atomic orbitals can be excited and leap up into empty orbitals of higher energy. This 'high energy' state is short-lived and the excited electrons soon return to the more stable lower energy orbitals. As they jump back down they release energy which is given off in the form of light. The energy spacing between different orbitals in different atoms is a known, quantized amount and consequently the energy or colour of the light given out is specific to the atom that has been excited.

Sodium lamps contain sodium in the form of a vapour, across which a very high voltage is applied. This starts an electrical discharge and the sodium atoms become excited and give off energy as yellow light, with a wavelength centred around 589nm. Many yellow street lights use sodium vapour. So why do some street lights appear red when they are first switched on? This is because a sodium lamp also contains a small amount of neon which is present to help generate heat and to warm up the metallic sodium atoms. So, the initial red glow of a sodium street lamp is due to the electrical discharge in the neon gas.

Since only specific energy levels of the atoms used in these lamps can produce light and the energy gaps between orbitals are element specific, the colour of the light emitted by each sort of lamp is like a fingerprint for the element used inside it. For example, neon produces red light and sodium produces a yellow light. So we can see that each type of electric light produces a distinctive spectrum and that each element in the periodic table gives off characteristic emission lines which can act as a fingerprint for that particular element. The light from a tungsten light bulb takes the form of a continuous spectrum and is due to the metal filament glowing white hot. The light spectrum from a quartz-halogen lamp differs from that of a normal incandescent light bulb because of the temperature of the filament, but the spectrum is still a continuous one. The colours of other lamps such as sodium and neon are due to specific atomic energy transitions and tend not to take the form of continuous spectra but appear as single or multiple coloured lines. Xenon lamps, sometimes found in laboratories, produce a combination of bright lines and a weaker continuous background spectrum, with different proportions of visible and infrared light compared to a light bulb or a quartz-halogen lamp.

So, to summarise, incandescent bulbs, mercury lights, fluorescent tubes, metal halide lights, sodium and neon lights can all be distinguished by studying the exact composition or spectrum of the light that they give out. This reflects the chemical elements that are used inside the lamps to generate the light.

The Flame Test

One of the simplest experiments for discovering the identity of a metallic element using light is the flame test.

Equipment required
A Bunsen burner
Platinum wire with a wooden or glass handle
A number of small crucibles
Metallic salts in powder form, eg salts of lithium, sodium, cobalt, strontium and barium
Ethanol

An inert platinum wire is cleaned in alcohol and heated in a Bunsen flame until it glows red hot. It should then be allowed to cool briefly before being wetted in ethanol and dipped in a small powdered sample of the metallic salt. The wire is then held in a blue Bunsen flame and the resulting flame colour can be used as an indication of the element in the powdered sample. For example, sodium salts give a yellow flame, cobalt salts give a blue flame, lithium salts give a crimson flame and strontium salts give a red colouration. The energy from the Bunsen flame excites the metal atoms which then give off this energy as light of a specific colour. This simple test is the basis of a useful branch of analytical science called flame emission spectrometry. The use of light in analysis is termed spectroscopy. At least 45 elements may be identified by their emitted light.

An alternative presentation for the flame test is to use small crucibles containing a small volume (5–10ml) of ethanol into which a small amount of the metal salts have been dissolved. If these crucibles are lit in a dark room the flames will clearly show the different colours associated with the metal salts. The salts of some metals are poisonous and should be disposed of with care.

Identifying Light Sources

As should be evident from the previous sections, most sources of light, whether they be street lights or flame tests, depend on the chemical constituents that generate the light for their coloration. This fact may be used to 'analyse' the light source and identify the elements from which it is generated. This doesn't require an expensive spectrometer as it is now possible to obtain high quality diffraction gratings and to use them for some simple but interesting experiments. Cheap diffraction gratings may be purchased through Edmund Scientific and single grating units mounted in a 35mm slide holder cost as little as 50p each, if bought in bulk (contact details for suppliers of equipment are given on page 119).

These small gratings are simply plastic films onto which a pattern of closely spaced lines has been impressed and which acts in the same way as the glass prism when held up against the eye and used to view a bright light source (see page 14). With these simple gratings it is possible for a class of pupils to carry out some very interesting science.

Light and Colour

> *Equipment required*
> Diffraction gratings
> Various light sources (such as tungsten light bulbs, fluorescent tubes, neon and sodium lamps)

Some of the light sources mentioned above should be set up so that pupils can view them through their diffraction gratings. Other room lights should be dimmed. The grating should be held in front of the eye with the edge of the slide mount touching the eyebrow. In the grating it should be possible to see, in addition to the light source itself, dispersed spectra spreading out to the left and right side of the light source. These should be identical and arise because of the way the grating is made. These spectra can be noted down and compared.

The spectrum of a light source can also be permanently recorded onto colour film for subsequent discussion and comparison. The requirements for these experiments are shown in figure 4 below.

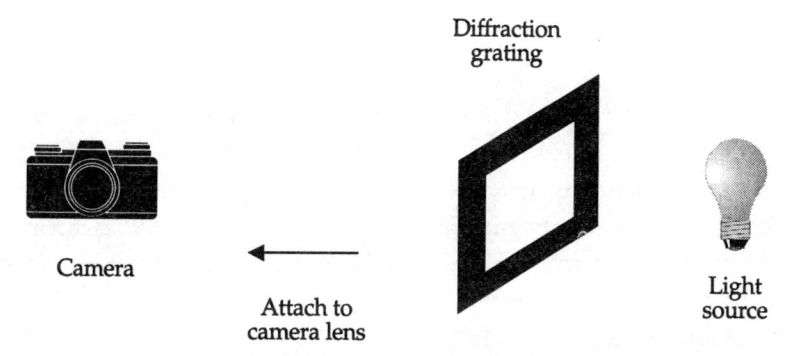

Figure 4

Camera ← Attach to camera lens — Diffraction grating — Light source

> *Equipment required*
> A grating
> A camera (any camera will do but a 35mm SLR is most suitable)
> A roll of colour film (ISO 400 or 800)
> A camera tripod

The grating, long side uppermost, is fixed with sticky tape over the lens of the camera so that the dispersed spectrum of a light source can be recorded onto the colour film. A Polaroid instant camera with colour film will also produce acceptable results which can be seen straight away. Single lens reflex (SLR) cameras are ideal since the spectrum can be viewed through the viewfinder before the picture is taken and this makes the apparatus simpler to set up.

Street lights, car headlights and lights in buildings and shops make excellent sources for recording and analysing and will all provide differing spectral patterns, and will indicate the type of lamp and its chemical make-up. Obviously, the best time to try this is when it is dark outside. Car stop lights making use of tungsten bulbs are beginning to be replaced by light-emitting diodes made of semiconductors such as gallium arsenide. These are highly efficient light emitters but have different spectral characteristics to the bulbs they replace. These patterns may be compared with the images of light bulbs or discharge tubes photographed in the classroom.

It is possible to obtain discharge tubes containing different gaseous elements. These are simply narrow glass tubes in which an electrical discharge can be stimulated by applying a high voltage from a power supply. Edmund Scientific have a power supply available for about £150 and tubes containing elements including hydrogen, helium, neon, bromine and iodine may be purchased separately for about £18 each. Spectrum analysis charts are also available which can be used when comparing the emission from these tubes (contact details for suppliers of equipment are given on page 119).

Other Sources of Light

The sun should not be stared at or photographed. However, on nights with a bright moon it is possible to get a record of the light which comes from the sun by looking at the sunlight reflected from the moon. Some method for stabilising the camera will be needed since the low light levels from the moon will require a long exposure time. This could mean propping the camera up on a table or a wall, or using a tripod or clamp stand. A fast film of at least ISO 400 should be used to ensure acceptable exposure times.

Other interesting results may be achieved with the use of a tripod. It is possible to enter the world of astrophysics by photographing bright stars on a clear night with a fast film and a zoom lens. Scientists use basically the same equipment (only many times more sensitive) to study the temperature and chemical make-up of the stars in our night sky. This is possible because stars act as intensely bright light sources, giving out a wide spectrum of colours.

As mentioned earlier, the colour of a hot body will depend on its temperature. Since stars are intensely hot, they emit spectra which are characteristic of their temperature and astronomers can measure the brightness of a star at many different wavelengths to make an accurate estimate of its surface temperature. For example, the sun emits light with a peak at around 510nm and this can be related theoretically to a surface temperature of approximately 5700°K.

This may be visualised simply in a laboratory by heating a piece of iron in a Bunsen flame until it glows white hot. The colour changes which are seen before the metal reaches this colour reflect the temperature changes that have occurred. Heating it to red heat, above 500°C, means that it is emitting light with a peak wavelength of around 700nm. Heating it further shifts this peak wavelength from 700nm to about 630nm as the metal becomes orange and by the time the iron is glowing yellow, the emission wavelength has moved to about 580nm. As the heating continues at above 1000°C the iron will eventually give out most colours of the spectrum, thus appearing to glow white. It should be remembered that most of the light being emitted by a red or white hot piece of metal cannot be seen since it is in the infrared part of the spectrum. However, it can be felt as heat (this is also true of the sun of course).

If a star has a surface temperature of 2000–3000°K, it will appear red. One such red star is Betelgeuse in the constellation of Orion. If a star has a temperature of about 6000°K, it will appear yellow. If it is near 10,000°K, it will appear white and above this temperature, it will start to appear blue-white.

Astronomy

So spectroscopy can tell astronomers the temperature of a distant star. But it can also tell them much more. A hot star emits an almost continuous light spectrum, from the ultraviolet through the visible to the infrared. As this light moves out and away from the star, it passes through the star's cooler atmosphere. This may contain gases of many different elements. These elements will absorb and block out specific colours of light from the continuous spectrum coming from the star. These elements will become visible from Earth from the black absorption lines superimposed on the star's continuous emission spectrum. As with emission, the absorption spectrum of each element is unique. So the black line (or missing) spectrum will tell scientists which elements are present in the cooler outer layers of the star. The intense heat and energy coming from the star can also act a bit like a Bunsen flame in the flame test and vaporise other elements in the star's atmosphere. These elements will appear as sharp lines in the star's spectrum. Gas clouds close to stars can be excited in a similar way and they too will emit light spectra. These can be used to look for complex molecules in faraway galaxies.

As an example of the importance of spectroscopy in astrophysics, American scientists have reported the discovery of acetic acid in an interstellar cloud 25,000 light years away from Earth using the professional equivalent of the demonstration described on page 21. Other examples of spectra which are seen in space are dark absorption bands caused by water vapour or ice (at a wavelength of 6.1 micrometres in the infrared region of the spectrum), methanol (at 6.8 micrometres) and methane (at 7.6 micrometres). These peak positions are known from experiments carried out on Earth, which have been designed to help scientists assign spectra from distant stars.

Light can also tell us other things. It can tell us how old a star is, whether it is travelling towards us or away from us and how fast it is

Light and Colour

going. From these facts much of the history of the Universe has been pieced together. Although much of what we know about astronomy comes from looking at visible light, many objects in the universe also emit energy at wavelengths that are even shorter than the ultraviolet or longer than the infrared. A great deal can also be learned from looking at these wavelengths which are invisible to the eye.

Web sites

There are a number of web sites that describe astronomy and stars:

- a three-dimensional star catalogue and star map can be downloaded from: http://www.maths.tcd.ie/~jaymin/chview/
- astronomical spectra from stars can be found at: http://www.achilles.net/~jtalbot/data/index.html
- there are two excellent web sites with guidance on photographing stars and some very good photographs at: http://www.snapnet.com/HVAG/articles/photo/photo.html and http://www.shef.ac.uk/uni/union/susoc/cass/homes/me/me931599/howto.html

The Department of Industrial Technology at Bradford University has set up an unusual web site at: http://www.telescope.org/. It allows users to log onto a robotic telescope and actually control its observations. The telescope is situated on the West Yorkshire moors. This site allows you to register as a telescope user and an observation request must then be submitted. Due to the popularity of the site the whole process can take a little while, but it is a very exciting use of the Internet and one which the University of Bradford is trying to expand by working with schools to provide similar telescopes around the world. Other automated telescopes may be found at the University of Iowa and at the University of California. Details of these and other web sites are listed on page 106.

Parallax

Parallax is used subconsciously by everyone with two eyes in order to judge distance and to help coordinate hand movements. It is also used

Demonstrations and Experiments in Science

by astronomers to measure how far away stars and planets are from the Earth. To do this, measurements are made of the angles subtended at the Earth's surface by these bodies. This process is repeated at a number of different points on the Earth, and by determining the distance apart that the measurements were made it is then possible to calculate their distance from Earth using simple geometry. However, parallax can also cause errors when reading scales on devices such as ammeters or voltmeters, so mirrors are placed behind the indicator needles so that the needle and its reflection can be lined up and parallax errors minimised.

Pupils should have an idea of the importance of parallax and should be able to devise a simple method for calculating the distance of objects using parallax, describe how our eyes use parallax to determine the distance of objects and make estimates of distances using parallax.

Equipment required
An overhead acetate
6 candles, placed on stools
A desk light
6–8 chairs
Metre rules

h = chairs   c = candles on stools   l = lamp

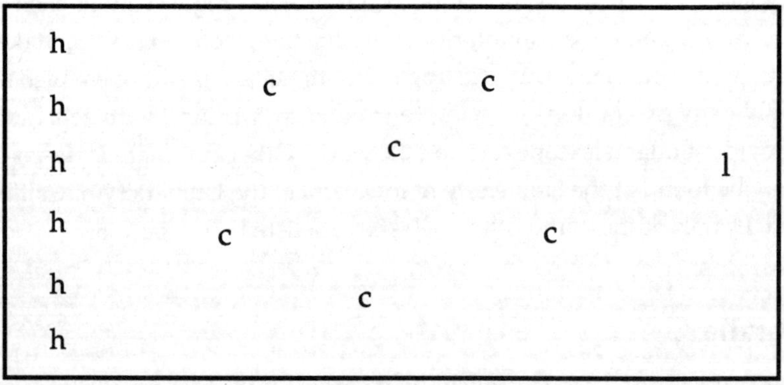

```
h
          c              c
h
                 c
h                                      l
h      c                    c
h
                 c
h
```

Figure 5

Take the overhead acetate, with a grid photocopied onto it (from graph paper) and then cut into long strips. In a darkened laboratory set out six candles on stools. They should not all be in a row, but fairly close, as shown in figure 5 opposite.

Place six to eight chairs across one side of the room and a small bright light, such as a desk lamp, at the other end. A pupil should sit in one chair and hold a piece of overhead acetate (with graph lines photocopied onto it) at arms length and close one eye. He or she should use this acetate to measure the relative distance between each of the candles and the light, and should record the data. The pupil should then move to another chair and repeat the measurement. He or she needs to record how far apart the chairs are from each other. The pupils should then get into groups of two or three and decide how to use the data in order to determine how far away each candle is. They are to assume the light is an infinite distance away (their answers will not be the same as the actual distances, as the light is not an infinite distance away).

The results should be compared and discussed. There are some other factors which should be taken into consideration. Do pupils have to measure the lengths of their arms? Did it matter which chairs they used, or how long their arms are? How does parallax help us determine how far away things are when we look at them?

Light Scattering

John Tyndall (1820–1893) was an English scientist who investigated light scattering. In studying how and why particles scattered light he provided an explanation for why the sky appears blue to observers on the Earth's surface. The Tyndall effect can be demonstrated in the classroom. The apparatus required and the set-up is shown in figure 6 (see page 28).

Demonstrations and Experiments in Science

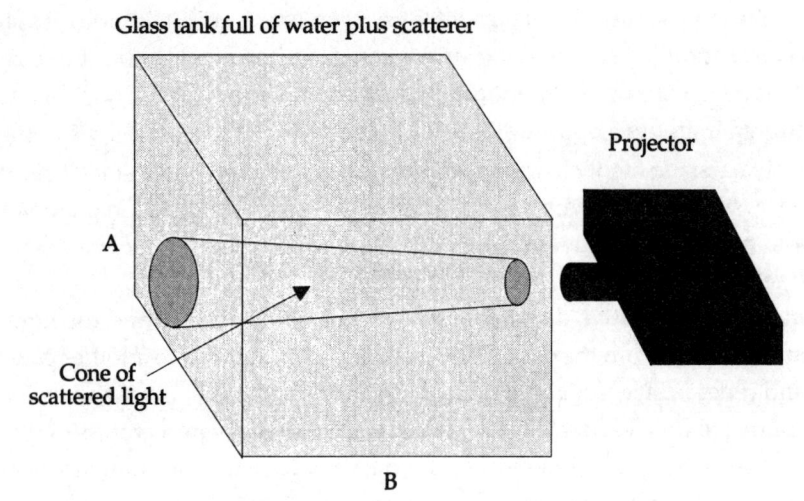

Figure 6

Equipment required
A slide projector
A small glass aquarium (1–4 gallons capacity) full of water
A screen or large mirror
For each gallon of water in the aquarium, you will need 20ml of saturated sodium thiosulphate (hypo) solution and 5ml of 6M hydrochloric acid

The aquarium should be set up almost full of water and the slide projector arranged to shine through the aquarium and onto a screen on the other side of the tank. The projector beam will be almost invisible where it passes through the water but will appear relatively bright and white on the screen placed on the other side of the tank.

Assuming the tank contains one gallon of water, 20ml of saturated sodium thiosulphate solution and 5ml of 6M hydrochloric acid are added and the water stirred. The water becomes turbid over a period of minutes as particles begin to be precipitated out into the water. These small particles begin to scatter the light and the projector beam begins to become visible as it passes through the tank and turns bluish. The light striking the screen becomes dimmer, turns slightly orange and the beam broadens in width. This may be seen when viewed from point A as shown in figure 6 opposite. Alternatively, a mirror may be used in place of the screen and then angled so that all the pupils can view the colour of the light striking it.

Very small particles or colloidal suspensions scatter light strongly but they do not scatter all colours of the spectrum to the same extent. When the particles are approximately the same size as the wavelength of light they begin to scatter the light but the intensity of this scattering is inversely proportional to the fourth power of its wavelength, hence blue (short wavelength) light is scattered much more than red (longer wavelength) light. Since the light from the projector contains all colours of the spectrum, we can see the scattering or Tyndall effect. The light being scattered by the suspension in the tank appears blue when viewed from point B in figure 6 while the light passing through the tank viewed at point A contains more of the colours which are scattered least and appears orange and red. The scattering also causes the projector beam to broaden.

The atmosphere contains many small particles of dust. When we look up we see a blue sky because much more of the blue component of sunlight is scattered than the yellow or red components. However, if you look directly towards the sun, at or around sunset or sunrise, the light is coming directly from the sun and so appears red or orange. These are the wavelengths which are scattered least and so more of this light reaches the eye. This effect is enhanced at sunrise or sunset because the light is passing through much more of the atmosphere than during the middle part of the day.

The water from the scattering experiment can be disposed of in a sink but care should be taken with the 6M hydrochloric acid used in its preparation.

Scattering From Particles

The scattering of light is also important in the visualisation of colours. Indian ink contains a very fine form of carbon suspended in a liquid such as linseed oil. This carbon is in the form of tiny carbon particles which are much smaller than the wavelength of light. They are so small that they do not reflect or scatter any light and thus appear black.

Another example of scattering used to produce colour has been revealed only recently. The Mayan Indians of Central America produced a bright blue colour on statues and sculptures called maya blue which has survived for centuries with almost no fading. In an attempt to understand how an ancient civilisation achieved such a long-lasting colour, scientists have recently analysed it and have discovered that it isn't a simple pigment but actually contains tiny particles of metal. These appear as a bright blue colouration because of their size. They, in a similar way to the sky, scatter only blue light. This ancient technology is now being looked at by paint manufacturers all over the world for modern applications.

Interference

Interference of light occurs under many conditions. The most famous example is Newton's Rings, an experiment which uses a convex lens placed on top of a flat glass plate. Light is reflected from the upper side of the plate and from the lower surface of the lens. The two groups of reflected light waves interfere with each other and produce rings of light and dark constructive and destructive interference.

Bubbles are also able to produce interference due to the extreme thinness of their walls, which are of the order of the wavelength of light thick. In this case, reflections from the inside and the outside surface of the bubble wall will interfere with each other. The two groups of reflected light waves travel different distances and if this distance is an exact number of wavelengths of a particular colour, then they will constructively interfere and create bright light of that colour. If they are out of step by an odd number of half wavelengths, the light will destructively interfere and the area of the bubble will appear dark. Because the thickness of a soap bubble is constantly changing, the colours that appear in its walls also constantly change. Bubbles are also great fun to play with so they make an ideal demonstration of interference, in conjunction with simpler demonstrations such as Newton's Rings.

Equipment required
Bubble solution
A lorry or tractor tyre
Wire (3 metre length)

There are a number of different recipes for making long-lasting bubbles. Standard soap bubble solutions are available commercially (which won't produce the best bubbles). A better option is to use a detergent (US types are recommended, such as Dawn or Joy) mixed with a small amount of glycerin (4:1 by volume of detergent:glycerin is good but the exact ratio can be experimented with). Alternatively, a complete home-made solution contains 3g triethanolamine, 4g oleic acid and 200ml of glycerol. This should be dissolved in 2.5 litres of water.

An exciting way of showing bubbles involves using a large tyre such as a lorry or tractor tyre, cut in half so it acts as a semi-circular trough. This is then filled with the bubble solution. A large circular wire frame is fashioned so that it can be dipped into the bubble solution inside the half tyre. This is the giant bubble maker. The wire frame should have a handle to allow easy control. A pupil can stand in the middle of the tyre and with practice, and the right detergent mixture, the wire ring can be lifted rapidly out of the bubble solution and a bubble will form around the pupil. Smaller wire rings can also be used with buckets of detergent solution to create huge bubbles. As the bubble films age, they tend to become thinner and the interference effects change. Eventually they will appear dark when they become too thin to allow constructive interference.

Thin film interference can be observed in a number of other items, including the inside of some large shells. Here, very thin layers of reflecting mineral act like the bubble wall, causing interference effects to occur between light from different surfaces. The eyes on peacock feathers are also caused by interference — not from thin films but from the fine feathers acting like diffraction gratings. Compact discs will also provide a similar effect (see page 14).

As well as thin film interference, soap bubbles are an interesting way to study geometry. Bubbles tend towards the most stable configuration and will always try to minimise their surface area, subject to the wire frame they are made on. Free floating bubbles will form a sphere, thereby minimising their surface area.

Equipment required
Modelling clay
Short wooden sticks (8-10cm long)
Detergent solution (see page 31 for details)

To investigate this further, the pupils can begin by constructing different shapes (squares, rectangles and boxes) using small lumps of modelling clay at the ends of short wooden sticks. When dipped in a detergent solution the bubble films will form the most stable configurations, which will not necessarily be the same as the shape of the frame.

POLARISED LIGHT

Light beams can be thought of as sinusoidally varying electromagnetic waves. These waves normally oscillate in all planes at right angles to their direction of travel. In this case, the light is termed 'unpolarised'. Daylight is one example of unpolarised light. However, as mentioned later in the section on laser light (see page 51), some forms of light have a specific direction of polarisation. Laser light is often polarised or unpolarised light from a light bulb can be turned into polarised light using a sheet of Polaroid. Polaroid may be purchased in large sheets from some optics suppliers and cut to size with scissors. Polaroid contains molecules which are all aligned in a single direction and only let light through which is

Light and Colour

polarised in this direction. Polarised light is very useful and is vital for many areas of research and industry (see page 34).

Polarisation by Scattering

Since scattered light from sand or from the sea is polarised, Polaroid is used in sunglasses to reduce glare. A demonstration to show the polarisation of scattered light is shown in figure 7 below.

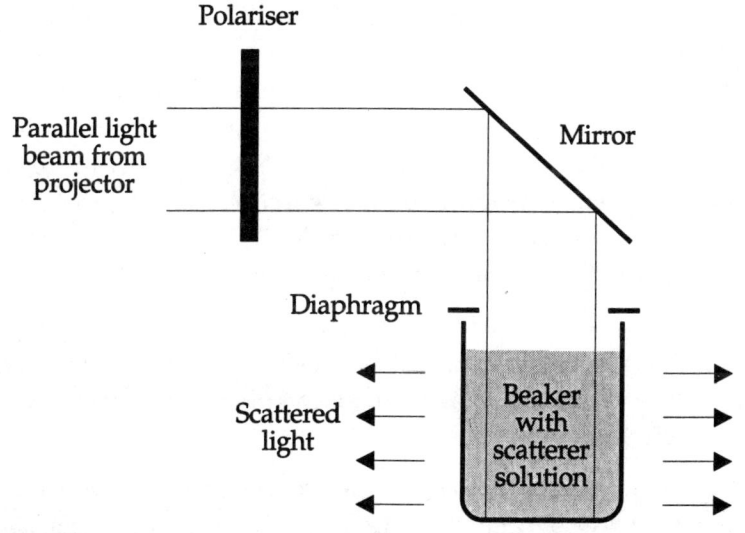

Figure 7

Equipment required
A bright light source, such as a projector
A mirror
A large glass measuring cylinder
Water
Milk or other scatterer
A piece of Polaroid film
A diaphragm
A quartz plate

A beam of light from the projector is arranged so that it forms a parallel or slightly convergent beam and is reflected downwards into a glass cylinder of water containing a scatterer such as milk (about 0.5ml of milk per 1.5 litres of water). The path of the light beam should be restricted by a diaphragm on top of the measuring cylinder so that the beam is confined within the sides of the glass cylinder and does not scatter from the sides. Scattered light should be seen in all directions horizontally. A mirror may be placed around the back of the cylinder so that the scattering is more visible. If a large piece of Polaroid film is placed in the light beam just before it enters the cylinder, it can be shown that the scattered light is polarised. The Polaroid should be placed in position and then rotated. The scattered light will be brighter when the light is polarised in one particular direction rather than another. As the polariser is rotated, the maximum and minimum intensities will be seen in the scattered light. The scatter is brighter in the direction perpendicular to the plane of polarisation and very faint or absent in the direction parallel to it.

Introducing a thick quartz plate between the polariser and the diaphragm will produce scattered coloured light. This is because the Quartz plate will separate the coloured components of white light and each will scatter differently.

This demonstration can also be carried out on top of an overhead projector. A piece of card which has a hole cut in it slightly smaller in diameter than the glass cylinder should be placed on the projector. The cylinder is placed over the hole and the Polaroid is placed beneath it. As before, the scattered light will change its intensity when the Polaroid is rotated.

Stress Birefringence

Polarised light is important in liquid crystal displays and is also used by engineers, who can use it to analyse the stress patterns in materials such as plastics. This is easy to recreate as a demonstration.

Light and Colour

> *Equipment required*
> An overhead projector
> 2 pieces of Polaroid film (about 12cm square)
> Various shapes, such as hooks, squares and circles, cut from a thin sheet (at least 5mm thick) of transparent plastic such as perspex (these should be slightly larger than the pieces of Polaroid)

A piece of Polaroid film is laid on top of an overhead projector. Onto this is laid a piece of perspex and then the other piece of Polaroid is placed over the top of this. The piece of perspex should be flexed slightly and the top Polaroid rotated until stress lines in the perspex become visible. Two pairs of hands are probably required to achieve this. When stressed, plastics can become birefringent. This means that they transmit one polarisation of light differently from other polarisations. The induced birefringence in stressed plastic is not noticeable under normal daylight but if polarised light is shone onto the plastic the birefringence becomes visible in the form of stress lines. These stress patterns are often seen in moulded plastics such as those inside layered car windscreens and are useful to engineers because they enable areas of high and low stress to be seen clearly. Items can be redesigned so that stresses are minimised or so that the plastic is made thicker or stronger in regions of higher stress.

Rotation of Polarisation

A solution of sugar acts as a birefringent material and rotates the plane of polarisation of light passing through it. This birefringence appears as spirals of colours.

> *Equipment required*
> A light projector with a bright bulb
> A glass tank or trough at least 30cm long
> A saturated sugar solution made from 400g of sucrose per 400ml of distilled water (enough solution must be prepared to fill the tank) ➤

> 2 large pieces of Polariod film
> A white screen
> A thick quartz plate
> Lenses
> A diaphragm made of black card

The tank should be filled with the saturated sucrose solution and the projector and lenses aligned so that the light forms a parallel beam as it passes through the tank. If necessary, the diameter of the beam should be limited with a diaphragm, made of black card, as it enters the tank. One of the pieces of Polaroid is placed in front of the tank and the polarisation of the light going into the sucrose solution can be adjusted by rotating this Polaroid. Since the sucrose solution is birefringent it will rotate the angle of polarisation of the light passing through it by an amount which depends on the exact concentration and path length of the sucrose solution. Since the rotation is different for different wavelengths of light there is rotational dispersion and different colours are seen along the tank, producing a spiral pattern. The reds and blues are most noticeable. As the polariser is rotated, the spiral will be seen to rotate. The separation of the colours may be made more pronounced if a quartz plate is inserted into the light beam before it reaches the tank.

To measure the degree of rotation, the second piece of Polaroid (the 'analyser') should be placed after the tank and a lens used to focus the light coming through it onto a white screen. Rotating the piece of Polaroid will make the image on the screen become brighter or darker. At maximum brightness the 'analyser' is aligned with the polarisation of the transmitted light. The angle of the analyser should be compared to the angle of the polariser on the other side of the tank to determine the degree of rotation. This is easier to do if the pieces of Polaroid are mounted in rotating holders which have degree markings on them. This effect will be more clearly visible with an intense light source such as an arc lamp.

> *Equipment required*
> An overhead projector
> 2 tall glass beakers (one filled with water, the other with saturated sucrose solution)
> A piece of card
> 2 large pieces of Polaroid film

An alternative set-up involves an overhead projector and tall glass beakers. A piece of card should be cut so that it fits onto the projector but has two holes cut in it slightly smaller in diameter than the beakers. One of the beakers is filled with water and the other with the saturated sucrose solution. A piece of Polaroid is placed beneath the beakers on the projector and the other piece is held above them. By rotating the piece above them, the beaker containing the sucrose solution will be seen to change colour. No effect will be seen in the beaker containing just water. This occurs because the sucrose solution rotates light of different colours to varying degrees. Shorter wavelengths are rotated more than the longer wavelengths. If one colour, for example orange light, is rotated 40° by the sucrose solution, the light coming out of the second piece of Polaroid will appear orange when it is rotated to 40° compared to the piece of Polaroid beneath the beakers. At the same time, if blue light is rotated by 70° as it passes through the sucrose, none of this colour will pass through the second piece of Polaroid when it is set to 40°.

All of these effects occur because of the nature of the sucrose molecule. Sucrose molecules are not symmetrical: they have 'handedness' in much the same way that our right and left hands are not identical. They are termed 'optically active' and interact with light by rotating it in the same direction. A solution of sucrose molecules, therefore, causes the polarisation of light to rotate.

Ice Lens

This is an interesting demonstration which is fun to experiment with and which may cause a few surprises.

> *Equipment required*
> 2 large watch glasses
> Distilled water
> A deep freeze
> 2 frames to hold ice lenses
> An arc lamp
> A match
> A piece of black paper

Fill the two watch glasses, about four inches in diameter, to the brim with freshly boiled distilled water and place them in a deep freeze to make two plano-convex ice lens. After they have frozen, slip them, with or without the watch glass lenses, into frames that have been prepared for them. These should be large enough to hold them against each other, flat-side against flat-side, to form one large biconvex ice lens. Introduce the lens into a beam from an intense light source such as an arc lamp and focus the light upon a match head, which should light, or onto a black piece of paper, which should start to smoke. The ice cell will last longer in the beam if a water cell is placed between the arc lamp and the ice lens as this will absorb all of the infrared radiation.

REACTIONS OBSERVED BY COLOUR CHANGE

Colour is vitally important in chemistry and is not just a by-product. It plays an important role as an indicator of the state of a reaction or of the pH of a solution. Life would be considerably more drab if it hadn't been for the chemistry of the dye manufacturers who have developed a wide range of bright and long-lasting colours.

Coloured Fountain

This demonstration shows the high solubility of some gases in water and the effect they have on the pH of the water.

> *Equipment required*
> A source of dry ammonia gas (or hydrogen chloride gas)
> An indicator solution, such as phenolphthalein
> A round-bottomed 1 litre flask with bung with two holes in it
> A 2 litre beaker
> A dropper with tightly fitting teat
> Glass tubing about 15cm long and 5mm internal diameter
> Glass tubing about 5cm long and 5mm internal diameter

The demonstration should be carried out in a fume cupboard since it involves toxic gases. The bung is placed in the round-bottomed flask and the longer piece of glass tubing inserted through one of the holes so that it almost reaches the other side of the flask. It should extend out of the flask at least 9cm.

The dropper should be inserted a very short distance through the other hole and the teat attached to the outside end. The flask is then positioned upside down above the large beaker so that the long length of glass tubing sticking out reaches almost to the bottom of the beaker. The apparatus should be held in position with ring stands and clamps.

The flask should then be filled with ammonia by the downward displacement of air. This can be done by carefully loosening the bung and pushing a length of hose into the top of the flask. This should be attached to a source of ammonia gas such as a cylinder. When the flask is full of ammonia, the hose should be removed and the bung carefully refitted. The dropper and teat should be removed and filled with a few millilitres of water and carefully replaced through the bung. Finally, the beaker beneath the flask should be filled with water containing a few drops of phenolphthalein indicator. When ready to start, the teat should be squeezed, releasing the water from the dropper into the flask itself. A little ammonia in the flask will dissolve in this water and the gas pressure in the flask will fall below atmospheric pressure. This will force the water in the beaker up the glass tube and into the flask. As it enters the flask like a fountain, the water takes up some of the ammonia and its pH changes, turning the indicator purple.

Ammonia is highly soluble in water. Another suitable gas for the fountain demonstration is hydrogen chloride, for which a suitable indicator would be bromothymol blue.

What can go wrong?
Gas leaking from the flask may prevent the fountain effect. A round-bottomed flask should be used since its shape gives it strength against implosion. A safety screen should be used or if carried out in a fume cupboard, the safety sash can be lowered.

Chemical Indicator

This is an example of a redox reaction, with the oxygen dissolved in the water oxidising the Indigo Carmine indicator to a green colour.

Equipment required
Two 1 litre flasks
Solution A: 7.5g of solid sodium hydroxide dissolved in 0.25 litres of distilled water
Solution B: 5g of glucose dissolved in 0.75 litres of distilled water
Indigo Carmine indicator
A beaker

The two solutions should be made up in two 1 litre flasks. Warm solution B to 38°C and add a small pinch of Indigo Carmine (disodium salt of indigo 5–5 disulphonic acid). This should be enough to give the solution a slight blue colour. Pouring solution A into solution B should cause the mixture to turn from blue to green. After a few minutes, the colour of the mixture should change from green to red to yellow. By pouring this mixture vigorously (from a height of at least 60cm) into an empty beaker, the colour of the solution should return to green. After an interval it should change from green to red to yellow once more.

These colour changes occur because as the dissolved oxygen in the solution is used up by the reaction, the indicator goes from a green to a red to a yellow colour. Re-introducing oxygen into the liquid by pouring the mixture from a height will cause its colour to return to green. This reaction is used to analyse the amount of dissolved oxygen present in boiler feed water. Pouring the water from a height causes re-oxygenation. Shaking the flask will achieve the same effect. Care should be taken with disposing of the sodium hydroxide solution but the chemicals can be disposed of safely after dilution with water.

The Clock Reaction

The clock reaction is so called because, by varying the concentration of the reactants used, a colour change may be made to occur at an exact time after mixing, after anything from 5 seconds to 45 minutes or longer. There are two main types of oscillating reactions:

(a) biochemical clocks, which are those involving enzymes and

(b) chemical clocks, which rely on a chemical change rather than enzyme action.

One of the best known chemical clock reactions is the Llandolt iodine clock. In this reaction, the final colour change is triggered by a sudden increase in the concentration of tri-iodide ions in the mixture. The reaction is analogous to a titration of iodate and bisulphite ions, with starch present as an indicator of the end point.

There are many variations in the chemicals used and the concentrations required. The following is a version used by Dr Brian Iddon and Bill Coates at The Royal Institution.

> *Equipment required*
> 12 test tubes
> Two or three 1 litre conical flasks
> Distilled water
> Potassium iodate
> Sodium hydrogen sulphite
> 10% sulphuric acid
> Soluble starch
> Solution A: 2.1g of potassium iodate, 10ml of 10% sulphuric acid in 1 litre of distilled water
> Solution B: 0.9g of sodium hydrogen sulphite, 4g of soluble starch, 10ml of 10% sulphuric acid in 1 litre of distilled water

By mixing the two solutions at differing concentrations (diluted with distilled water) the reaction forming a dark blue complex may be made to occur at different times as indicated below:

- 100% A + 100% B: time = 5 seconds
- 50% A + 50% B: time = 25 seconds
- 40% A + 40% B: time = 57 seconds
- 30% A + 30% B: time = 1 minute 40 seconds
- 25% A + 25% B: time = 2 minutes 50 seconds
- 20% A + 20% B: time = 45 minutes.

The exact clock period (the time between mixing and colour formation) depends on the initial concentrations of potassium iodate and sodium hydrogen sulphite, the temperature of the mixtures and the pH of the solutions. Increasing the initial concentrations or the temperature, or reducing the pH, will reduce the clock period.

There are a number of different ways in which the clock reaction can be presented in the classroom. All solutions can be added in synchronisation, and a stop clock started. In addition, the temperature of solution A can be adjusted or concentrations varied, which will change the resulting clock time. A simple but effective demonstration may be made by lining up between five and 10 beakers and, starting at one end, mixing the reactants into the beaker and moving immediately to the next one and so on. If the timing is right, by the time the reactants in the last beaker have been mixed, the first beaker will react to become dark blue. All of the rest will follow in sequence.

Although a bit too theatrical for many people, this reaction can also be "performed" to a suitable piece of music, such as the 1812 Overture or even something more modern. A number of different solutions at differing concentrations can be made up to change at pre-selected times, matching changes in the tempo of the music.

The solutions are hazardous and should be disposed of by dilution with water. The dark blue complex can be rendered colourless by stirring with sodium thiosulphate. The sodium hydrogen sulphite can release sulphur dioxide under some conditions, which can cause breathing difficulties. Avoid contact with skin.

Belousov-Zhabotinsky Reaction

This chemical reaction is named after the two Russian scientists who investigated it in the 1950s. It is actually a class of oscillating reactions, involving repetitive colour changes in a solution which take the form of colour waves moving through the liquid. The time which the reaction lasts for and the rate at which the colours change depend on the exact mixtures used. There are many variations. These colour changes are the result of competing reactions in the chemical mixture. Which reaction is occurring at any one time is controlled by a chemical (which itself is produced or consumed in these reactions) whose concentration acts to 'switch' or control which of the pathways is dominant.

Shakhashiri (1985) has a detailed section describing this class of complex reactions (see page 118). Two variations are described below.

Demonstrations and Experiments in Science

Version 1

> Equipment required
> 5 500ml flasks
> A measuring cylinder
> Solution A: 0.43g of cerous nitrate in 500ml of distilled water
> Solution B: 14.3g of malonic acid in 500ml of distilled water
> Solution C: 26.1g of potassium bromate in 500ml of distilled water
> Solution D: 500ml of 1.5M sulphuric acid
> Solution E: ferroin solution, prepared by dissolving 0.23g of iron (II) sulphate (heptahydrate) in 100ml of distilled water and then adding 0.46g of 1, 10-phenanthroline (not the hydrochloride salt)

The solutions should be prepared in 500ml flasks. Equal volumes of solutions B, C and D are mixed carefully in an ungraduated measuring cylinder and then a few millilitres of solution E added. The same volume of solution A is then poured in slowly down the side of the measuring cylinder so that it doesn't mix completely with the other solutions. Different coloured stripes will slowly appear and disappear over a period of many minutes.

Version 2 (after Shakhashiri)

> Equipment required
> 4 500ml flasks
> A 1 litre beaker
> A magnetic stirrer
> Solution A: 5g of potassium bromate dissolved in 250ml of 0.9M sulphuric acid
> Solution B: prepared by dissolving 6g of methyl malonic acid in 250ml of distilled water and then adding 1.2g of potassium bromide
> Solution C: 1.7g of cerium (IV) ammonium nitrate dissolved in 250ml of 0.9M sulphuric acid
> Solution D: ferroin solution prepared by dissolving 0.23g of iron (II) sulphate (heptahydrate) in 100ml of distilled water and then adding 0.46g of 1,10-phenanthroline (not the hydrochloride salt)

Light and Colour

These solutions should all be prepared in 500ml flasks. Solutions A and B should be mixed in a 1 litre beaker about 30 minutes before the demonstration and stirred with a magnetic stirrer until they become colourless. Once this has happened, solution C and 15ml of solution D should be added. Over a period of minutes, the colour of the solution will start to change from green to blue to violet and then to red. This change will cycle for hours, gradually slowing down. These reactions can be presented on top of an overhead projector to make them more visible.

What can go wrong?

On the whole, these reactions are rather temperamental. The beakers and flasks used for the reactions must be extremely clean and the water and chemicals pure since some contaminants such as chloride ions can inhibit the colour changes. These reactions are also sensitive to temperature. Care must be taken with the sulphuric acid, the malonic acid and the bromate, none of which should be allowed to come into contact with the skin. The mixtures can be disposed of after neutralisation with an alkali such as sodium bicarbonate.

Chemiluminescence

Chemiluminescence is a term used to describe light that is given off by a chemical reaction. The most common reaction used in the laboratory to demonstrate chemiluminescence involves the use of luminol or 3-aminophthalhydrazide. Luminol may be made to glow by oxidation. There are a number of possible oxidation systems which can produce different colours. See Shakashiri (1985), Iddon (1985) and Taylor (1983) for possible mixtures.

If reacting luminol to create light is too complex or time consuming, a simpler way of demonstrating chemiluminescence is with the use of light sticks, which are cheap and widely available. These are made by Cyalume (American Cyanamid Company) and typically do not use luminol but hydrogen peroxide and an oxalate ester. These react together and transfer chemical energy to a dye which subsequently emits this energy as visible light. A detailed discussion of the chemistry of chemiluminescence may be found in *Chemical Demonstrations: A Handbook for Teachers of Chemistry* (Shakhashiri, 1985). Light sticks are used for fishing or for emergency lighting by walkers, yachtsmen and many others, and may be purchased in the UK from Miltrain Ltd (for address see page 120).

Chemiluminescent light sticks are sold in sealed foil packets since they are moisture sensitive. However they will last a long time if the foil wrapping is undamaged. Removing the foil reveals a plastic tube containing the reactants. The chemical reaction is started by bending the tube until a slight snap is felt. This breaks open a glass vial that is inside the outer plastic tube and which contains some of the chemicals. When the tube is shaken, the chemicals are mixed and the chemiluminescent reaction begins to emit light. The rate of reaction depends on the temperature of the reactants, and while the specifications for the light stick will indicate the amount of time that useful levels of light are given out for, the reaction rate can be changed by heating or cooling the light stick. Placing it in ice-cold water or in the freezer will reduce the reaction rate, dim the light given out and extend the lifetime of the light stick, while heating it in a beaker of warm water will enhance the brightness of the light, which will be given off for a shorter time. By changing the temperature of the light stick and measuring the relative light levels given out it is possible to obtain an Arrhenius plot and determine the activation energy for the chemiluminescence reaction. Shakhashiri measured it to be 56.4 kJ/M between -5°C and 50°C.

Chemiluminescence Reactions

There are numerous recipes for creating chemiluminescence in the laboratory. Details of three versions are given here.

Light and Colour

Version 1

> **Equipment required**
> A 5 litre flask and a glass funnel
> A glass tube
> Two 2 litre flasks
> Solution A: 0.2g of luminol and 20ml of aqueous sodium hydroxide (5%), diluted to 2 litres with distilled water
> Solution B: 0.5g of potassium ferricyanide, dissolved in 20ml of hydrogen peroxide solution (3%), diluted to 2 litres with distilled water

The two solutions are made up in the 2 litre flasks and mixed simultaneously into the 5 litre flask in a darkened room. The resulting mixture glows brightly. Alternatively, a glass tube may be fashioned into a long spiral. With the funnel in the top of this tube, and the bottom placed into the 5 litre flask, the two solutions can be poured simultaneously into the funnel and will glow brightly as they run down through the glass spiral. This makes a very impressive reaction in the dark.

Alternatively, the potassium ferricyanide may be left out and after mixing the two solutions, a few drops of blood squeezed from a piece of raw liver will also start the chemiluminescent reaction. Care should be taken with the chemicals used in this reaction and they should not be allowed to come into contact with the skin.

Version 2

> **Equipment required**
> Two 1 litre conical flasks
> 1 litre of distilled water
> A 2 litre beaker
> A glass tube
> A large funnel
> Solution A: 4g sodium carbonate, 0.2g luminol, 24g sodium carbonate, 0.5g ammonium carbonate, 0.4g of copper (II) sulphate pentahydrate ➤

Demonstrations and Experiments in Science

> Solution B: 50ml of hydrogen peroxide (3%), diluted to 1 litre with distilled water

Both solutions should be dissolved in 1 litre of distilled water in a 1 litre conical flask. Mixing solutions A and B in a 2 litre beaker in a darkened room will make the mixture give out a blue chemiluminescence. Alternatively, as described on the previous page, a glass tube may be fashioned into a long spiral and carefully clamped in position above the beaker. With a large funnel in the top of this tube, and the bottom placed into a 2 litre beaker, the two solutions can be poured simultaneously into the funnel. They will glow brightly as they run down through the glass spiral.

Version 3

> *Equipment required*
> A 500ml flask
> 200ml of dimethylsulphoxide (DMSO)
> 20ml of 3M potassium hydroxide solution
> 0.1g of luminol
> 0.02g of disodium fluorescein

DMSO is an extremely hazardous, toxic chemical and must not be allowed to come in contact with bare skin. It should not be disposed of down the sink. The DMSO is poured into a 500ml flask and the potassium hydroxide, luminol and fluorescein added. The chemiluminescence is started by aerating the solution by shaking it. This will cause a bright yellow glow to occur. As the oxygen is used up, the glow will fade. It may be made to re-appear by shaking the flask.

What can go wrong?

All of these reactions use chemicals, such as DMSO, hydrogen peroxide or sodium hydroxide, which can cause burns to skin. They should be used

Light and Colour

carefully and protective eye-wear and gloves should be worn. These chemicals can be disposed of after dilution with large volumes of water.

A chemiluminescence Internet homepage set up by the chemistry department at Sam Houston University in Texas may be found at http://www.shsu.edu/~chm_tgc/chemilumdir/chemiluminescence2.html.

Chemiluminescent Clock Reaction

This clock reaction, also described by Shakhashiri, should be carried out in a darkened laboratory. The end point of the time period is marked by a blue luminescence.

Equipment required
2 100ml volumetric flasks
A 1 litre volumetric flask
A magnetic stirrer
10 beakers
Solution A: 0.08g of DL-cysteine (hydrochloride hydrate) dissolved in 50ml of distilled water in a 100ml flask
Solution B: 5g of solid potassium hydroxide dissolved in 100ml of distilled water in a 100ml flask, then 0.1g of luminol added and dissolved by swirling the flask
Solution C: 0.25g of copper (II) sulphate pentahydrate dissolved in 50ml of distilled water; dilute to 100ml, and then transfer 25ml of this solution into a 1 litre volumetric flask and make it up to the 1 litre mark with distilled water
3% hydrogen peroxide solution

To present the reaction, five beakers should be placed on magnetic stirrers and into each should be measured 5ml of solution A and 5.5ml of solution B. A magnetic stirrer bar should also be added. Just before the reaction is started, 40ml of solution C should be measured into five other beakers, together with 0.5ml of fresh 3% hydrogen peroxide solution.

With the stirrers on and the lights dimmed, one by one the beakers containing solution C and the hydrogen peroxide should be added to the beakers sitting on the stirrers. The clock period for the mixture should be approximately 45 seconds. Blue light will be emitted sequentially from the beakers in the order in which the solutions were mixed. The clock time may be varied by changing the amounts of cysteine, copper sulphate or hydrogen peroxide used. Increasing the amount of copper sulphate or hydrogen peroxide will reduce the clock period and increasing the amount of cysteine hydrochloride will lengthen the time before final reaction occurs, for example a 30 second clock period can be obtained using 60ml of solution C or 0.1ml of hydrogen peroxide, with all other amounts being equal.

What can go wrong?

The solutions should be made up freshly for the demonstration as the clock reactions will not occur if the solutions are too old. The timings will be wrong if concentrations are not accurate and the temperature of the solutions are different.

Care should be taken with all the compounds and solutions above, since all can be dangerous in one form or another. Hydrogen peroxide can act as a bleach and can give off oxygen. Copper sulphate dust is an irritant and the dangers of both luminol and cysteine are unknown at present. If small amounts are used and they are diluted well with water, all the chemicals can be safely disposed of in a sink.

Triboluminescence

This is a form of luminescence generated by mechanical force. It involves the release of stored energy, held in crystal structures as light energy in the form of photons of emission. A simple way of observing this is to use zinc sulphate crystals. If these are ground using a glass pestle and mortar in a darkened room, small flashes of light are observed as the sliding friction that occurs as the crystals are ground releases energy from the surfaces that are sliding or being ground over each other. Another way of demonstrating this is to snap cooled Polo mints in the dark. Small flashes of light are given off as the mints are broken but these are very weak and can only be seen if looked at very closely in a dark room.

LASERS AND LASER EXPERIMENTS

In the last few years, there has been a proliferation of suppliers of inexpensive lasers and optics (a selection of which are listed on page 119). These changes have been accompanied by improved reliability. It has never been easier to construct experiments and demonstrations to illustrate the principles and applications of lasers.

Laser Light

A laser is simply a device that produces a special kind of light whose properties and behaviour differs markedly from the light of, for example, a light bulb. The word 'laser' is an acronym, standing for Light Amplification by Stimulated Emission of Radiation. The point of note here is that a laser is simply a light amplifier, acting upon light in an analogous way to a hi-fi amplifier on electricity. However, the light that is produced by the amplifier (known as the laser beam) has a number of unique properties. Laser light typically consists of only one colour (it is monochromatic), unlike the white light emitted by most light bulbs. Laser light is also capable of being focused into narrow beams that have little divergence and are able to travel, as a thin beam, for extremely long distances. Laser light can also be extremely intense.

The way in which laser light is formed means that it has very different properties to the white light from, say, a torch. Using an analogy with sound, white light is similar to the noise that we hear in the street, a jumble of interfering sounds and pitches. The light from a torch or candle appears to be white but is actually a mix of different colours or wavelengths, travelling in different directions. This sort of light is called incoherent light. Laser light is coherent and, continuing the analogy with sound, is like a pure musical tone, consisting of a single colour. This is termed monochromatic. This difference may be shown using a powerful torch, a prism and a red laser. Shine the torch through the prism and a multicoloured spectrum will be seen on a piece of card held on the other side. However, shining the laser through the prism will only produce a single spot of red light. Coherent light is light in which all of the waves travel in phase with each other and are all of the same wavelength. The difference between incoherent and coherent light may be likened to an audience clapping at random compared with a regular synchronised clapping.

The directionality of laser light can be illustrated by shining a torch and the laser along a laboratory and measuring the size of the light spot on a screen. The torch beam is highly diverging, while the laser produces only a small spot.

Another important property of laser light is its extreme intensity. Since all of the light energy is concentrated into a narrow beam, it is possible to use a laser's power to cut through steel. A 60W light bulb gives out its light energy in all directions, making it useful for lighting the home but a 60W laser represents a powerful source of energy, with all of the photons, or packets of light, travelling in a narrow beam perhaps only 2mm in diameter. To gain an idea of the intense nature of a laser beam, the bright output of a 1mW laser beam should be compared with a 10W light bulb.

Its great intensity and small divergence means that laser light will travel for long distances and still be bright. The distance between the Earth and the Moon has been accurately measured by aiming a laser beam at reflectors placed on the Moon's surface. The time taken by the light to reach these mirrors and be reflected back gives us a direct measure of distance since the speed of light is known.

Buying a Laser

Many types of lasers are available and the number of options is increasing rapidly as technology advances. Those most commonly on sale differ in a number of ways. The older generation of teaching lasers are gas filled helium/neon lasers, which typically cost in the region of £200 and upwards. Whilst these lasers have a number of useful properties, making them good for teaching in schools, they are becoming increasingly outdated and expensive, as a new generation of tiny, solid-state diode lasers have arrived on the market. The development of these new lasers has been spurred on by the communications industry where, with such large profits at stake, advances in design and reductions in price have been rapid.

Diode lasers vary in the wavelength of light that they can produce, the power of this light and hence their 'class' and their safety designation. Class 2 semiconductor lasers, which are safe for use in schools and which can be powered by a small battery, can now be purchased for under £50 and prices are still falling.

Useful diode lasers operate at wavelengths from about 670nm to 635nm. Lasers with a wavelength of 635mm are newer and therefore more expensive. The wavelength is important since it will affect how visible the laser beam will be in the classroom. The eye has its peak efficiency between 500nm and 600nm so for a given output power, the shorter wavelength laser beams will be more visible to students. A low power (1mW) diode laser working at 670nm may cost in the region of £50, a 1mW diode laser operating at 650nm may cost around £60 while a diode laser working at 635nm giving the same power may cost about £100.

Although price will probably be the main consideration when choosing the type of laser, the advice of the National Radiological Protection Board should also be taken into consideration. They recommend the use of a class 2, 1mW, 635nm diode laser. These will seem as bright to the eye as higher powered lasers working at 670nm. So, while purchasing a cheap, high powered diode laser working at 670nm may initially seem the best option, it could actually represent a greater danger to eyes if not used with care. The laser classification of any diode lasers should be checked before purchase. Details of recommendations can be found in

British Standard BS EN 60825, *Radiation Safety of Laser Products* (see page 111 for more information on laser classification).

Diode lasers can be purchased in the form of pen laser pointers with built-in battery power supply or as diode laser modules, without the power supply. Since the laser pointers are made for a mass market, they are very cheap and may be a very good buy, costing typically around £40 for 5mW 670nm laser. However, it should be noted that these lasers and are not recommended for use in schools (although they are fine, apparently, as lecture pointers). Especially good value are the cheap Russian laser pointers now being imported into this country.

Alternatively, unpackaged diode laser modules may be built into experiments more easily than laser pointers and a DC power supply, connected to the mains supply will reduce battery costs if the laser experiment is to be heavily used. Typically, the supplies required for diode lasers are between 3V and 6V and need fairly low currents of, for example, 70mA, so a simple circuit can be built quite cheaply or bought ready assembled.

Another important consideration is the beam divergence of the laser, which should be checked in its specification before purchase. This is a measure of how much the laser beam spreads out with distance. This may be given as around 0.5–1.5 milliradians or may be described as a fan angle. Diode lasers tend to have quite large divergence compared to helium/neon lasers but this is easily corrected by purchasing a small lens which may be mounted on the front of the laser. These small corrective lenses are fairly cheap. It is perhaps best to buy diode lasers that have a small lens already built in. Another consideration before purchasing is the polarisation of the laser light. Diode lasers do not always produce polarised light — again, check the specification. This will be important if experiments are going to be carried out which investigate the properties of polarised light.

Alternatively, a simple piece of Polaroid film, placed in front of the laser, will give the beam sufficient polarisation and will not reduce the beam brightness significantly. Even with a lens and Polaroid included, these diode lasers are still considerably cheaper than most helium/neon lasers (though even these can now be obtained for less than £100 in kit form). Optics and kits can be purchased cheaply from the suppliers listed on page 119. For some special uses such as holography, a stabilised helium/neon laser is recommended.

Laser Demonstrations

The rest of this section gives details of demonstrations that may be used to complement other teaching material and which should enhance pupils' interest in, and understanding of, optics, light and lasers. Beyond key stage 2, lasers may fit into a number of science study programmes including the application of science and the nature of light. Their use can also fulfil a number of roles within a design and technology course.

Laser beams can be dangerous if viewed directly into the beam, so care must be taken with all of these demonstrations to avoid such a possibility. The lasers and optics must be properly mounted in strong rigid mounts. Back or stray reflections should be noted and blocked, as near to their source as possible. Some authorities recommend that demonstrations should be carried out with the laboratory lights on, since in the dark eye pupils will be dilated and eyes will be more susceptible to damage should a stray beam hit them. The issue of laser safety is considered more fully on page 111.

Total Internal Reflection

There are a number of different ways in which lasers can be used to demonstrate the phenomenon of total internal reflection (TIR) at an interface. TIR can be shown at a water/air interface with the use of a laser and a clear-sided tank of water. This demonstration is shown in figure 8 overleaf.

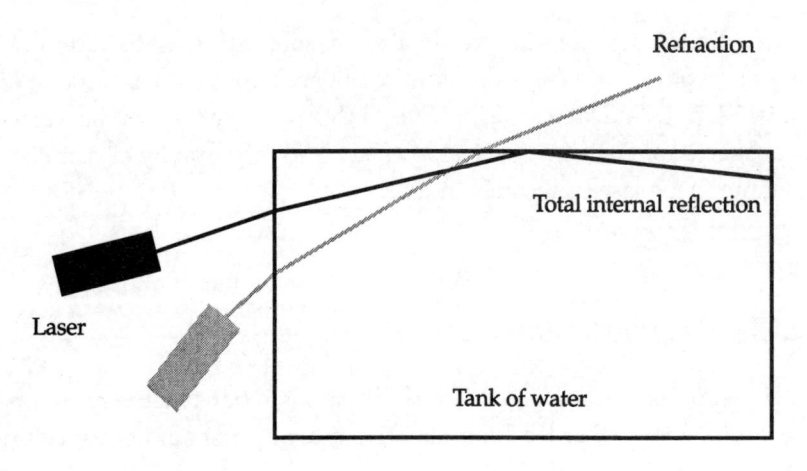

Figure 8

Equipment required
A laser
A clear-sided tank filled with water
Milk

The laser is placed low on a bench by the side of the tank and aimed upwards into the tank so the beam strikes the water surface from underneath and at a glancing angle. The resulting reflection back into the tank shows TIR occurring. This is shown in the diagram by the dark lines. By lowering the laser and changing its direction, the angle of incidence at the surface may be made steeper until, at less than the critical angle, TIR no longer occurs and the laser beam is refracted upwards out of the tank. The laser beam may be made to show up in the tank by adding a small amount of milk to the water, but care must be taken with this demonstration since there will be stray reflections from the tank and the water surface. Measuring the critical angle can then allow the calculation of the refractive index of water (n=1.33). The critical angle for water is about 49°.

A simple way of illustrating TIR in an optical fibre is as follows.

Light and Colour

Equipment required
A laser
A solid glass rod
A white screen
A bowl
A funnel

Use a short length (up to 60cm) of solid glass rod about 1cm in diameter which has been bent into a gentle 'S' shape and which has clean, polished ends. Shining a laser into the end of the rod results in most of the light coming out of the other end, as viewed on a white screen. When viewed from the side, it can be seen that very little escapes out of the sides of the glass rod. Light is bouncing along inside the rod because of the difference in refractive index between the glass and the outside air.

A further demonstration of TIR uses a jet of water instead of a glass tube. This is shown in figure 9 below.

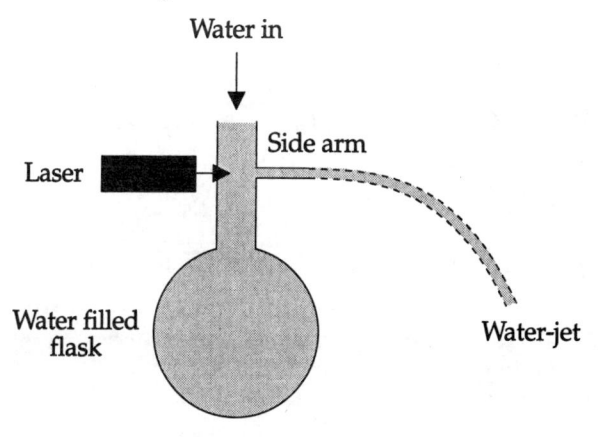

Figure 9

Equipment required
A laser
A glass flask with a side arm
A source of water

The flask should be set up with clamps by the side of a sink so that it may be constantly topped up with water and so that the jet of water leaving the side arm is caught in a bowl in the sink. A funnel should be placed in the top of the flask to help keep the water level in the flask above the side arm so a constant water jet is produced. The initial lining up of the laser should be made with no water in the flask. The laser is mounted with clamps so that it shines through the neck of the flask and out of the side arm, parallel with the path of the jet of water. Care must be taken in lining this up since back reflections may be unpredictable. The laboratory lights should be dimmed. When the water is introduced to the flask, a jet of water will constantly flow out of the side arm and into the bowl. When the laser is switched on, its light beam is guided down the curving jet of water, lighting up the water as it falls into the bowl. If the jet is interrupted with a finger, the light may be seen on the skin. This experiment can be lined up using a bright torch as the light source before the laser is switched on.

What can go wrong?

Care must be taken not to get water on the laser. The flow of water into the flask must not be so vigorous as to cause bubbles which will interfere with the laser's path.

Modern telecommunications rely heavily on the use of lasers beamed along optical fibres over long distances. A slightly more advanced demonstration can show how voices may be transmitted along optical fibres via modulated light.

Equipment required
A fibre optic audio link kit
A length of plastic optical fibre

This involves buying a simple kit (eg Maplin fibre optic audio link) and will also require a length of plastic optical fibre (this can be anything from

Light and Colour

a few centimetres to several metres in length, although beyond 10 metres the signal may start to degrade). It is constructed so that at one end of the fibre is an encoder circuit with a small infrared light-emitting diode (LED). This is mounted on a small printed circuit board powered by a 5V battery supply. By connecting a microphone to this end, the voice of a volunteer or music from a radio is converted into an electrical signal, which is encoded or transmitted into the infrared light beam. This modulated light is then sent down the length of plastic optical fibre, which may be up to 20 metres long, on a 110kHz carrier signal. At the other end of the fibre is a decoder or receiver circuit using a small photodiode detector, which requires a 9V battery supply to power it. This decoder circuit picks up the modulated speech on the light beam carrier signal and converts it from light intensity fluctuations into a varying electrical signal. This electrical signal is then converted back into sound. By attaching a small amplified speaker to this decoder end speech transmitted along the fibre may be heard. This apparatus is shown in figure 10 below.

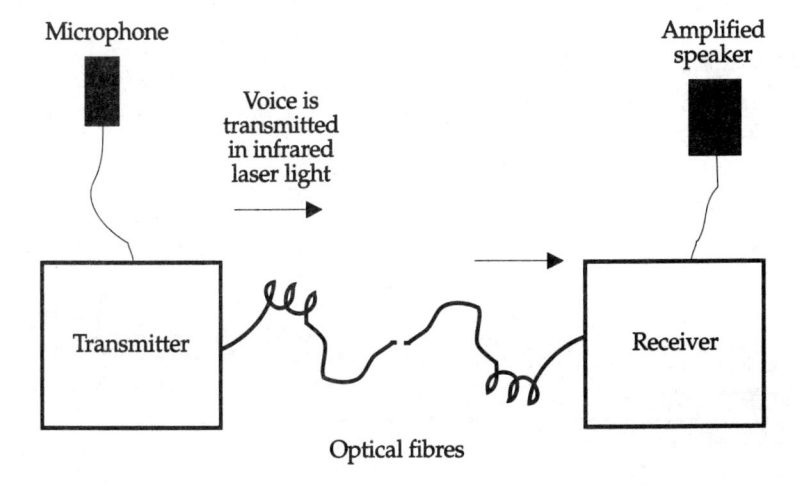

Figure 10

The low power infrared laser LED is invisible and safe. Transmission along the fibre may be shown by cutting (cleanly) the plastic fibre. Sound will even be transmitted when the ends are aimed at each other but not necessarily touching. Sound can also be received when the light is transmitted for short distances through water. This may be shown by putting both ends of the fibre into a glass or tank of water and moving them towards each other as someone speaks into the microphone. Both transmitter circuit board and receiver circuit board may be built into simple plastic boxes to protect the electronics. The complete kit is available from Maplin Electronics for under £30 and a complete constructed version is available from Edmund Scientific (see page 119 for contact details).

Measuring the Wavelength of Laser Light

For these experiments it is important to note that for an exact answer the laser must give out laser light of a well defined wavelength. If a helium/neon laser is used in the experiments, then the laser wavelength will be precisely 632.8nm because helium/neon lasers work at a well-defined value. However, diode lasers, unless they are stabilised, will produce laser light with a less well-defined wavelength. Typically, the quoted wavelengths for diode lasers are ±10nm. This extra error must be taken into account in the following experiments if diode lasers are used.

An important experiment is the classic Young's double slit experiment, which shows interference in coherent laser light.

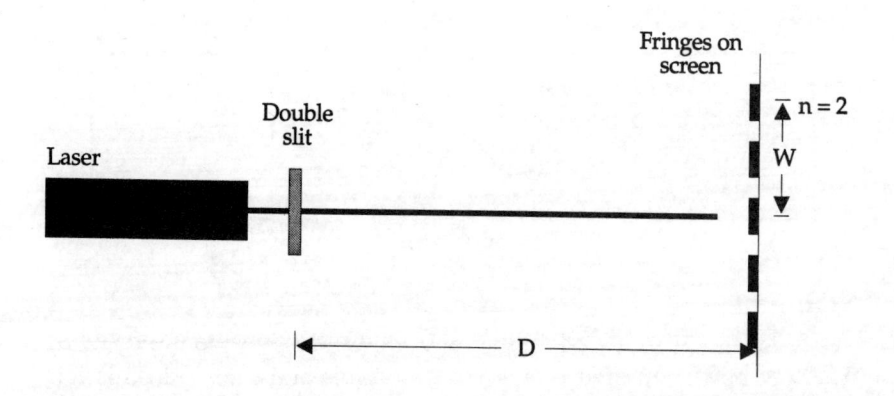

Figure 11

Light and Colour

> *Equipment required*
> A laser (ideally a helium/neon laser)
> A screen
> A double slit

A screen is used to observe the interference fringes generated when laser light is allowed to interfere. This is achieved by using a double slit (two closely separated slits) placed in the laser beam in front of the screen so that each slit acts as a separate source of light waves. Because the original laser light is coherent (ie of the same wavelength and with waves in phase) when two waves arrive at the screen any number of whole wavelengths out of phase, their intensities will add or constructively interfere. On the other hand, where a pair of waves arrive an odd number of half wavelengths out of phase (peak and trough coinciding) they will destructively interfere and cancel each other out. This produces a series of bands or fringes on the screen. The set up for this experiment is shown in figure 11 opposite.

By measuring the fringe and slit separations and the distance from the slits to the screen, it is possible to work out the wavelength of the laser light from the following equation:

$$nL = \frac{SW}{D}$$

where n = an integer
L = wavelength of the laser
S = width between slits
W = distance of the nth bright band from the central band
D = distance from the slits to the screen.

Commercial double slits are best purchased for this experiment, but if they are made then the separation may be measured using a travelling microscope. The laser should not be focused onto the slits. Separation between the slits and the screen should be at least 1 metre. The further away the screen is the easier it is to measure the fringe separation, but the dimmer the image will be. It should be possible to see up to 10 fringes on either side of the central one.

Another slightly different experiment which can be used to measure the laser beam wavelength utilises the millimetre scale on a metal ruler as a diffraction grating to produce interference. The use of a metal ruler as a diffraction grating is explained on page 14. It can also be used to measure the characteristics of the laser beam.

Equipment required
A laser
A metal ruler

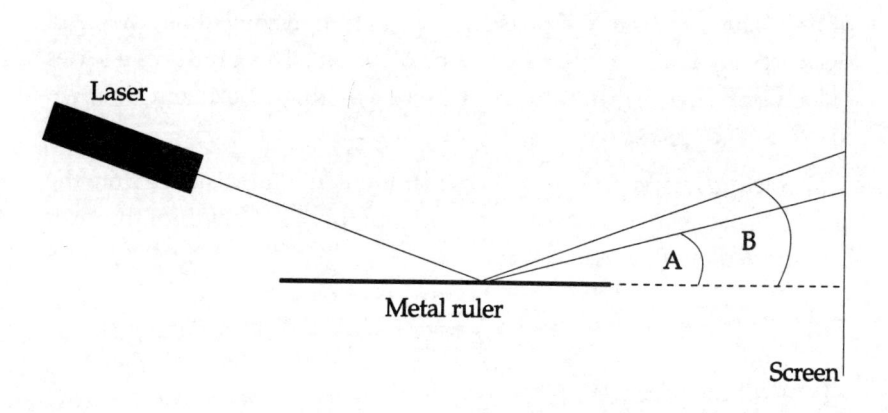

Figure 12

The laser is aimed at the millimetre scale of a metal ruler at a glancing angle and a screen arranged so that the reflection of the beam can be observed. This apparatus is shown in figure 12 above. Above this reflection it should be possible to see a series of spots due to the first and higher order diffracted beams. Up to 10 higher orders may be observed. These spots are caused by constructive interference between light diffracted from the markings on the ruler. Each of the rulings acts as a centre for

Light and Colour

diffraction. The two diffracted waves from a ruling will be in phase when the path difference between them is a whole number of wavelengths.

The position of the central reflection can be checked by moving the laser to an unruled point in the middle of the ruler. By measuring the incident and diffraction angles, together with the separation of the rulings (1mm), it is possible to calculate the wavelength of the laser light.

For constructive interference:

$$d(\cos A - \cos B) = nL$$

where: d = the separation of the rulings on the ruler
A = incidence angle
B = diffracted angle
n = an integer and
L = laser wavelength.

A and B can be calculated using trigonometry and measuring the positions of the diffracted and undiffracted beams and the distance between the ruler and the screen.

Listening Device

A complex but interesting demonstration is outlined in *Radio-Electronics* magazine (see page 119). It describes the use of a laser and the optical lever effect to eavesdrop on, for example, a ticking clock. This relies on the clock's ticking to produce vibrations in its glass cover. A laser beam reflecting from this glass cover vibrates at the same frequency as the ticks of the clock. By shining the reflected laser beam onto a light sensor, the motion of the laser beam is converted into an electrical signal which may be listened to using a speaker. This device could be used to listen to conversations behind a closed window since speech will cause a similar movement in the glass panes of a window.

CHAPTER 3

MATERIALS AND PHYSICAL PROCESSES

This chapter uses demonstrations and experiments to examine the properties and characteristics of polymers and non-Newtonian liquids, as well as detailing how to prepare polyurethane foam and polymeric sulphur, and illustrating the heat of crystallisation.

POLYMERS

Polymers are fundamental to our lives. They are incorporated into almost everything we use, from the clothes we wear (nylon, silk, cotton, etc) to most items that we use in the home or at work (such as plastics and rubber). It must also be remembered that all living things are made of polymers, our bodies are constructed from proteins (polypeptides) and sugars (polysaccharides) and our genetic code is contained within a polymer chain called DNA. Cellulose and the chemical components that make up wood, such as lignin, are the plant equivalents of our sugars and proteins. Oils, waxes, leather, wool and fur for clothing, canvas for sails, hemp and flax for ropes and paper have all been fundamental to the development of man and all are polymers.

So what is a polymer? The name comes from Greek, meaning 'many parts', and describes a large molecule which is made up of many single units, joined together one after another. These units may be atoms but more commonly are groups of atoms formed into a small molecular unit. How many of these single units (or 'monomers') are needed to form a polymer is an open question; some chemists would suggest that at least 100 monomers are required to be joined in a chain before a molecule becomes a polymer. Polymers can vary in size and be made up of anywhere between 100 units up to many millions of units. Polymers may also take many forms. The monomer units of a polymer may be identical or different, arranged at random or in a sequence. The polymer chains themselves may be isolated from one another in a dilute solution or they may be joined to each other by weak or strong chemical bonds, forming soft or hard materials. The possibilities are almost infinite and this fact explains the great versatility of polymer chemistry. Rapid advances in chemistry, physics, materials science and biological engineering mean that polymers are becoming even more vital in the world around us. The subject makes up an important component of the National Curriculum. It relates both to physical processes (forces and pressure on solids) and to materials and their properties (bonding and structure) at both key stages 3 and 4.

The Size of Polymers

As already mentioned, polymers are giant molecules made up of between hundreds and millions of monomer units. The average length of a polymer chain, together with the size and composition of its monomer units, will determine the molecular weight of the polymer, which, in turn, will determine many of its properties.

Large polymers made up of chains containing many thousands or millions of monomer units can produce solutions which are highly viscous. It is difficult to stir a viscous solution because of the great length of the polymer chain. Parts of the chain which are in static or slower moving areas of the solution tend to anchor the other parts of the polymer chain which are being stirred and this effect restricts motion. So one way of investigating the 'size' or molecular weight of a polymer chain is by

Materials and Physical Processes

measuring its viscosity in solution and by comparing this to the viscosity of other solutions or to that of the plain solvent itself. Whilst rigorous quantitative measurements are hard to achieve, a simple demonstration of the effect of polymer size on viscosity may be carried out fairly easily.

> *Equipment required*
> A small number of 200ml or 500ml measuring cylinders (500ml cylinders are larger and thus more visible) ideally made of clear plastic
> A variety of small spheres, such as ball bearings or small marbles
> Solutions of different viscosity, such as water, glycerin, hexadecanol, etc

This purely quantitative demonstration is one which can be adjusted to cater for pupils of different ages. A simple demonstration to convey differences in viscosity could involve dropping marbles into measuring cylinders containing liquids such as treacle, washing-up liquid and water.

Alternatively, a slightly more involved demonstration may be carried out involving timing the descent of the spheres from the top to the bottom of the cylinder. The same volume of each of the solutions are placed in the measuring cylinders and the spheres are dropped, one at a time, into the liquids and their descent, from the moment of release to the moment they reach the bottom, is timed. The more viscous the solution, the longer the spheres will take to fall and this may be related to the size of the polymer chains in solution. The rate of descent should be compared for a variety of liquids with known molecular weights and used, together with the time of descent, to predict the molecular weights of other liquids. Suitable liquids of known molecular weight can be purchased from chemical suppliers (see page 120 for contact details). If the liquids are safe, pupils can carry out the experiments themselves.

What can go wrong?

If the spheres are too heavy and the viscosity of the liquid is low, then the descent may be too rapid to measure accurately. Therefore, spheres of different weights should be available and used with all the liquids. If the spheres are heavy and they fall fast, they could even break a glass measuring cylinder. There are also other factors to be taken into account when analysing the experimental results, since interchain forces (attractive or repulsive) will modify the viscosity of the solution.

Rubber

Natural rubber had been used in small quantities by man for hundreds of years before the chemists of the last century discovered methods for processing it into an extremely useful material. Many kinds of synthetic rubbers have since been developed to replace natural rubber. Rubber is an ideal material to investigate in the classroom since it is safe, cheap and widely available and its properties may be the subject of a number of interesting demonstrations. Rubber is useful because it is elastic, hard wearing and impact-absorbing. All these properties arise from its chemical structure. In natural rubber, the monomer unit is called isoprene, and has the following structure.

$$-[CH_2-CH=C(CH_3)-CH_2]-$$

There are many kinds of synthetic rubber, such as polybutadiene and butyl rubber, which differ from each other in monomer structure but have similar general properties to natural rubber.

Why Does Rubber Stretch?

The best known property of rubber is that it is elastic. Early ideas of elasticity in rubber compared its behaviour with that of a spring. The behaviour of rubber was viewed in terms of a 'passive' model. However, this was inconsistent with some of its other properties. The origin of elasticity in rubber is actually kinetic.

Rubber is a polymer. It is its twisted and tangled polymer chain structure that is the key to why it is elastic. As the rubber is stretched, these chains begin to untangle and unwind, allowing a piece of rubber to extend by up to seven times its original length. When released, the rubber will contract back to its original size and the polymer chains will re-entangle themselves. However, there are some materials which have a tangled chain structure but which are not elastic. So, what is unique about rubber and why are rubber polymer chains tangled and twisted? As already mentioned, these chains are themselves made up of many single monomers. The atoms in these monomers are not fixed and stable but constantly vibrate and rotate with thermal energy. It is these motions which lead to the twisted, tangled structure of the polymer chains. This can be illustrated simply with a skipping rope.

Equipment required
A skipping rope (about 2 metres long)

The rope is spun by two pupils. As it is spun faster, they each should be able to feel that their end of the rope is beginning to pull inwards towards the other end. The motion of the rope swinging around and around pulls the two ends of the rope towards each other just as the motions of the atoms on the chains in rubber tend to pull the two ends of the polymer chains inwards. This results in the chains forming a tangled mass. Since rubber contains millions of these polymer chains, statistically at equilibrium, most of them will be highly tangled due to these motions. Rubber's elasticity is due to the extension of these tangled chains. When released, the vibrations and rotations of the chain start to act like the spinning skipping rope and pull the ends of the chain back towards each other, causing the rubber to contract again.

Maxwell's theory describing the distribution of gas velocities may be used to determine the distribution of end-to-end distances for a polymer chain.

The Thermo-Elastic Effect

This effect means that if the elasticity of rubber is due to thermal energy of the atoms on the polymer chain, then the elastic restoring force is

Demonstrations and Experiments in Science

proportional to temperature. This can be seen in the following demonstrations.

Equipment required
A rope
A metal sheet
A mallet or hammer

The rope is placed on a metal table (or a metal sheet laid on top of a wooden surface) and is laid out in short straight sections. This represents a section of rubber which has been stretched so that its polymer chains are untangled. Banging the metal table top with a large wooden or rubber mallet or hammer simulates adding heat into the system in the form of vibrational energy. The banging causes the table top to vibrate and the rope to move in a way analogous to that produced by heating the polymer chain. The movement and vibration causes the rope to start to move and as the table is struck it forms an increasingly tangled pattern. This illustrates that as energy is added to rubber in the form of heat it will increasingly try to contract by entanglement.

Alternatively, a more quantitative demonstration is possible.

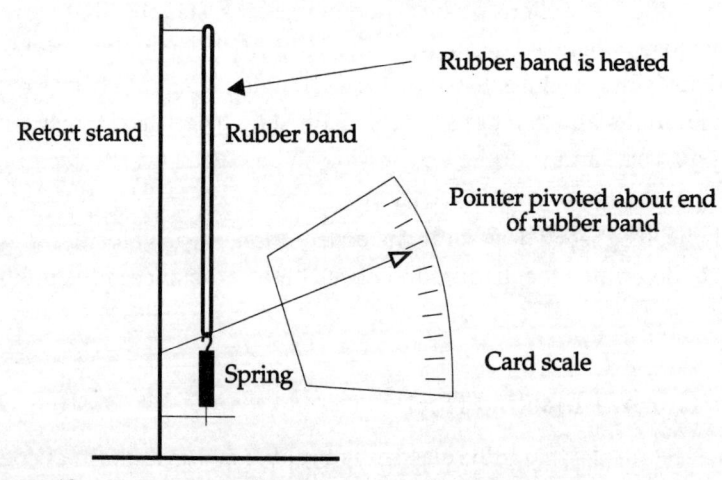

Figure 13

Equipment required
A rubber band (7.5mm thickness)
A spring
A retort stand and clamp
A beaker of boiling water or hot air blower
A long wire pointer

Attach a rubber band to one end of a spring. Attach the other end of the band to a clamp at the top of a retort stand. The free end of the spring should be clamped to the bottom of the retort stand so that the rubber band is tensioned by the spring. The temperature of the rubber band can be adjusted by clamping the retort stand so it hangs downwards from a lab bench and the end with the rubber band can be placed in a beaker of boiling water. This should be arranged so that it will heat the rubber band but not the spring. By attaching a long pointer made of light wire to the point at which the spring meets the rubber band and by pivoting it about a point close to where the rubber band and spring meet, the amount by which the rubber band contracts when heated by the boiling water can be determined. This arrangement is shown in figure 13 opposite. Alternatively, a hot air blower can be used to heat the rubber band. Since the rubber only contracts by a very small amount, the pointer should be long and attached firmly to both the spring and to the pivot. A suitable spring should be chosen to tension the rubber band so that small changes in its length will be evident.

The thermo-elastic effect can also be demonstrated very simply using a rubber band. Hold the elastic band against a sensitive part of skin such as the upper lip and stretch it suddenly. It can be felt to warm up and if it is held in extension and allowed to cool back to room temperature, then held again against the lip and allowed to relax suddenly, it should be easy to feel that the rubber band has cooled. If this stretching and relaxing is repeated several times, the heating and cooling cycle becomes easier to distinguish.

Note that there are strong parallels between the kinetic theory of gas and the kinetic theory for rubber's elasticity. Charles' Law states that the pressure of a gas at constant volume is proportional to its absolute temperature. Compressing a gas by doing work on it with an applied force generates heat. In the same way, doing work by extending a piece of rubber will generate heat in the chains as work is done to unravel them.

NON-NEWTONIAN LIQUIDS

Rheology is the science of flow and deformation of matter, and encompasses viscosity and the elasticity of substances. All materials deform to some extent when subjected to a force, be it fast stirring or just gravity. Liquids may be called Newtonian liquids if their viscosity does not depend on the stress or force that is placed upon them, ie slow or fast stirring or pumping does not change their viscosity. However, for liquids that contain large complex molecules, such as polymers, it is sometimes the case that their viscosity depends on the stress that is applied to them, ie the faster they are stirred the more or less viscous they become. These are called non-Newtonian liquids. Note also that their viscosity may go up or down as the stress increases. The rheology of liquids is of great practical importance. The design of pumps, mixers, extruders and moulds in many industrial processes will depend on the viscosity and elasticity of the liquid being made or used, and an understanding of rheology is important in the production of materials as diverse as toothpastes, plastics, greases, paints and motor oils.

There are many interesting examples and demonstrations of non-Newtonian liquids which are educational in a number of ways but also great fun to play with. The following demonstrations show the very different ways in which highly viscous polymer solutions can behave when compared to 'normal' liquids, such as water. They illustrate some of the properties of non-Newtonian liquids and may be used during the teaching of viscosity and intermolecular forces, as well as being interesting examples of liquids, polymers or materials. Specifically, this section

Materials and Physical Processes

fits into key stage 4 under forces and motion but is also relevant at key stage 3 when teaching centres on materials, since these polymers exhibit properties common to both solids and liquids alike.

Preparation of a Self-Siphoning Liquid

A solution of poly (ethylene oxide) acts as a non-Newtonian liquid. It will siphon out of a beaker even when the surface of the solution falls below the lip of the beaker. It can pull itself out completely. This effect is shown schematically in figure 14 below.

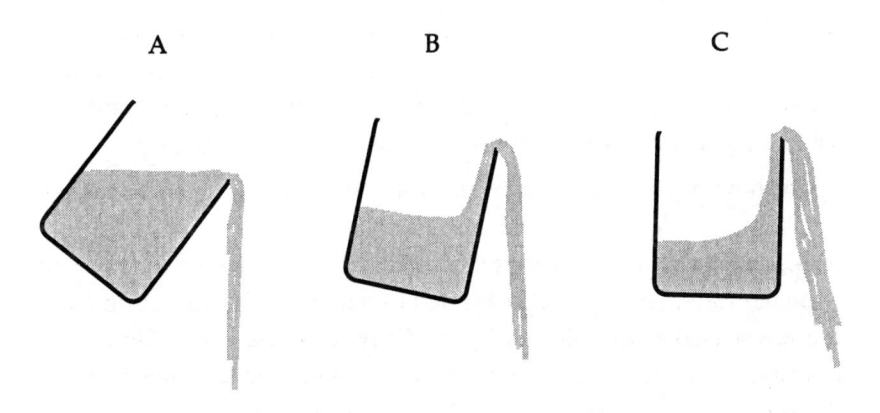

A   B   C

Figure 14

Equipment required
1.5 litres of distilled water
20ml of propan-2-ol (isopropyl alcohol)
Two 2 litre beakers
A 100ml beaker
A broad hand stirrer or spatula
12g of poly(ethylene oxide) of relative molecular mass of at least 4×10^6 (obtainable from Aldrich or from Union Carbide, where it is known as Polyox WSR-301) ➤

> An airtight bottle or jar
> A catcher tray
> Food colouring or dye

The polymer solution is made by placing about 12g of poly(ethylene oxide) into a 100ml beaker and adding enough propan-2-ol (10–15ml) to produce a suspension of the polymer. This is then added slowly to 1.5 litres of distilled water in a 2 litre beaker, whilst being constantly stirred with a broad stirrer or spatula. The stirring must be vigorous or the polymer suspension will form lumps and will be hard to dissolve. The poly(ethylene oxide) must have a molar mass of about 4 million g/M. The mixture must be stirred continuously for at least 15 minutes, then occasionally for about one hour. It is then best left in an airtight bottle or jar for one or two days before use to ensure complete solubility.

To show how highly viscous the polymer is and to demonstrate the open-siphon effect, the polymer solution should be placed in a 2 litre beaker on the edge of a bench with another 2 litre beaker on the floor (in a catcher tray). The top beaker is tilted to start the polymer pouring into the lower beaker (position A in the diagram on page 73). Return the pouring beaker to the upright position (position B in the diagram) and the polymer should continue to siphon out of the top beaker by itself (position C in the diagram). With practice, it is possible to get all of the polymer to siphon out. Food colouring may be added to the distilled water before adding the polymer to give the final polymer solution a bright appearance. Alternatively, dyes such as rhodamine 6G or fluorescein may be added. These can produce an impressive fluorescence from the solution in a darkened room if UV (black) lights are used to show off the polymer as it siphons. The polymer can be stored in an air-tight container for many months.

What can go wrong?

The polymer must be fully dissolved in the water and no lumps should be present. If poured too slowly, the self-siphoning will not begin and only some of the polymer will leave the beaker. If poured too fast, all the polymer will leave rapidly and this may be difficult to control and the demonstration will lose some of its visual impact. Spillage onto flooring or carpet will be a problem since the polymer is hard to clean up. Care should be taken to avoid this and the use of a large catcher tray beneath the lower beaker is recommended. The polymer should not be allowed to come into contact with the skin.

The polymer solution can be disposed of by dilution with large quantities of water and flushed safely down the drain. If dyes other than food colourings are added, the possible dangers of the dye used must be considered.

Rod-Climbing Polymer Solution

A Newtonian liquid will form a vortex when stirred fast, but stirring a non-Newtonian liquid results in rod-climbing. This can be illustrated with the following demonstration.

Equipment required
500ml of glycerol
5g of poly(acrylamide) of average molecular mass 5×10^4 g/M
A 1 litre beaker
A hot plate and a motor stirrer
A hand-cranked or variable speed mixer

500ml of glycerol should be warmed on the hot plate in a 1 litre beaker to about 35°C. The solid polymer is then added slowly into the warm glycerol and stirring is maintained for several hours with the glycerol maintained at about the same elevated temperature until the polymer is completely dissolved.

The solution should be allowed to cool. To demonstrate rod-climbing, a hand-cranked stirrer is placed in the liquid and as the solution is stirred, the polymer may be seen to climb up the crank of the stirrer. Alternatively, a variable speed mixture can be used. This effect may be compared to other liquids such as pure glycerol or water. This polymer solution consists of a greatly extended three-dimensional polymer structure with complex fluid properties. In fact, the same effect is observed when bakers stir dough (dough consists of a complex polymer structure of starch and sugars). Many liquids, including solutions of proteins or polymers, exhibit non-Newtonian behaviour such as the rod-climbing described here. This effect is illustrated in figure 15 below.

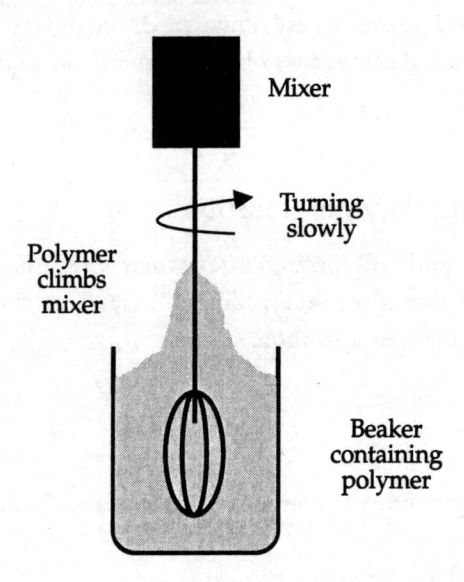

Figure 15

What can go wrong?
If the solution is overheated and stirred too vigorously the polymer can break down, changing the properties of the polymer completely. If the poly(acrylamide) is not fully dissolved then there will not be sufficient quantity in solution to form a full network and results may be disappointing. Be careful not to run the mixer at too high a speed or the polymer will get out of control.

The solution can be kept in an air-tight jar for repeated use and food colouring can be added to make the polymer visible. Disposal requires dilution with excess water and the solution may then be disposed of down a drain, followed by flushing with more water.

Preparation of an Elastic Liquid

This material has intermolecular forces which are intermediate between a solid and a liquid. Its properties can be shown using the following demonstration.

Equipment required
100g lauric acid
1 litre 0.75M sodium hydroxide solution (made with distilled water)
85g potassium aluminium sulphate dodecahydrate dissolved in 0.5 litres distilled water
20g phosphorus pentoxide
1 litre pure toluene
Glass beakers
A 2 litre jar
A filter
A pair of scissors

Mix the lauric acid with the sodium hydroxide solution in a beaker, warm to 50°C and stir until the liquid clears. Dissolve 85g of potassium aluminium sulphate dodecahydrate in 0.5 litres of distilled water and slowly add this to the sodium laurate, forming a white precipitate. Filter this and dry at 60–70°C for two to three days. Dry further over 20g of phosphorus pentoxide for about a week. Finally, place 40g of the dry aluminium hydroxydilaurate in 1 litre of pure toluene and shake the mixture (in a 2 litre jar) until a gel forms. Then shake periodically until the mixture becomes homogeneous. The mixture should thicken up. It is then ready for use. While pouring the gel from one beaker to another, the flowing liquid should be cut with a pair of scissors about 10cm below the spout from which it is pouring. The elastic liquid should stop flowing and rise back up into the top beaker. This demonstration requires practice to perfect.

What can go wrong?

Distilled water must be used for this preparation. The drying of the final aluminium hydroxydilaurate must be thorough or the gel will not form during mixing with toluene. The gel will not thicken if not thoroughly dried out and all water removed.

Sodium hydroxide is hazardous and will cause burns to skin, eyes, etc. Phosphorous pentoxide is also hazardous and must be treated with caution. Toluene is highly inflammable and a suspected carcinogen: use in a fume cupboard.

Preparation of Slime

Slime may be prepared by mixing polyvinyl alcohol with borax. This makes a gel which is soft like putty and which can flow very slowly, like a liquid, but which can be broken like a solid by stretching or bending it rapidly.

Equipment required
2g polyvinyl alcohol and 50ml warm water or 200ml Unibond glue
5ml saturated sodium borate solution (borax)
A beaker
A spatula

2g of polyvinyl alcohol are dissolved in about 50ml of warm water and then allowed to cool. When 5ml of a saturated sodium borate solution is added with stirring a gel forms. This should be stirred until a uniform mix is produced which should then be washed with water.

Alternatively, a white glue such as Unibond may be used. This is made of polyvinyl alcohol and is a simple alternative to making the solution up from scratch. Using a pot of about 200ml, the glue should be poured into a beaker. About 5ml of saturated borax solution is added and the glue is stirred with a spatula for about three minutes, until it begins to gel. A little more borax solution may be added to get the mix to the desired consistency. Note that over a period of hours the solidity of the slime will increase so it should be made of slightly softer consistency than that finally desired. The excess glue should now be washed from the slime and this should be repeated until the water is no longer white. Let the slime dry on a hard surface and after about 15 minutes the slime can be handled. It will become a more consistent texture if it is squeezed by hand for about 10 minutes. The slime will then flow slowly if left on a hard surface and if placed on top of a tin can it will flow down its sides in a couple of hours. It should bounce on a hard surface and, if pulled hard, the slime will snap like a solid.

The chemistry of slime formation is quite simple. The borate ions react with the hydroxil groups of the polyvinyl alcohol and cross-link the polymer chains. These weak cross-links can break and reform allowing the visco-elastic gel to deform and flow. This slime can be compared with bitumen or chewing gum. Borax is toxic and should not be swallowed. The gel can be coloured with dyes to make it fluoresce under 'black' lights.

OTHER DEMONSTRATIONS

Preparation of Polyurethane Foam

Polyurethane is a versatile polymer which is widely used for many applications. It is possible to make polyurethane foam by mixing equal parts of part A and part B of a commercial two part polyurethane foam mix. Part A typically contains a polyether polyol (a blowing agent to produce carbon dioxide gas to expand the foam), silicone surfactant and a catalyst. Part B contains a polyfunctional isocyanate. These are known commercially as Suprasec (isocyanate component) and Daltolac (polyol component). One manufacturer is ICI (see page 120 for contact details).

> *Equipment required*
> Part A and part B polyurethane foam mix
> 2 containers (plastic disposable cups or glasses are ideal)
> A large tray
> A stirring rod

Equal amounts of the polymer solutions are mixed together (typically 20–50ml of each) and stirred vigorously for about 30 seconds in a large disposable plastic cup. The container is placed on a tray and within a minute the reaction will begin and foam will start to bubble up and out of the container. Although the gas produced (carbon dioxide) is safe, the liquids are hazardous and should not be allowed to come into contact with the skin. Once the reaction has stopped, the foam will be warm due to the exothermic nature of the reaction and it should not be touched for two to three hours because of unreacted chemicals on the surface. It is best placed in a fume cupboard during this time.

In the foam reaction the polyol and the isocyanate react together to make a urethane polymer linkage, and the foam is expanded by a blowing agent. The amount of blowing gas produced and the degree of cross-linking in the polyurethane affects the final rigidity of the foam. This will affect its properties and uses.

There are six basic methods for foam preparation.

1. Physical incorporation of gas into polymer by mixing.
2. Chemically produced gas from reactions.
3. Volatilization of solvent, boiling off pentane in case of expanded polystyrene.
4. Blowing agents, eg chemical decomposition.
5. Syntactic foams, eg by incorporation of hollow microspheres.
6. Temporary fillers, removed afterwards by chemical leaching, eg soluble salts.

Methods 2–6 are used to produce fine control over the structure of the foam and the size and nature of the bubbles within it. Polyurethane foam

Materials and Physical Processes

may be blown by either the carbon dioxide formed during the side-reaction of the di-isocyanate with water or by the incorporation of halocarbon blowing agents in the polymer pre-mix. The polyurethane reaction described above uses method 2 for foam production.

Preparation of Polymeric Sulphur

Sulphur exists at room temperature in the orthorhombic form, as an eight membered 'crown' ring structure. If it is heated to above 170°C and poured into cold water, it forms a linear polymer with a molecular weight of millions. This plastic sulphur is stable only for a few days, after which it starts to revert to the more stable orthorhombic structure. The experiment should be carried out in a fume cupboard.

Equipment required
A Bunsen burner
Boiling tube and tongs
50–100g of flowers of sulphur
A 1 litre beaker of cold water

Sulphur is put into a boiling tube until it is about one third full. It is then held in a Bunsen flame and rotated until the suphur melts. The sulphur should turn to an amber coloured liquid. The heating is continued until the sulphur becomes dark red. At this stage the sulphur sometimes ignites. It will give off sulphur dioxide which is toxic and which should not be inhaled. The boiling sulphur should then be poured into a large beaker of cold water where it will cool immediately to form thin yellow threads of polymerised sulphur. This is sulphur in a polymeric form with a molecular weight of over a million. The properties of this 'plastic' sulphur should be compared to those of the stable form at room temperature.

Heat of Crystallisation

Crystallisation from a supersaturated solution of sodium acetate is an exothermic reaction and generates considerable quantities of heat.

Equipment required
100ml of distilled water
250 grams of sodium acetate (trihydrate)
A water bath heater
A 250ml flask
A bowl of cold water
A small beaker
A large petri dish

The sodium acetate is dissolved in the 100ml of distilled water in the 250ml flask over the hot water bath. This will require occasional swirling and when fully dissolved will produce a supersaturated solution. The flask can then be cooled by sitting it carefully in a bowl of cold water. The supersaturated solution should be handled carefully and allowed to cool completely undisturbed, with a small beaker placed over the neck of the flask to prevent dust getting onto the solution. Once cool, the solution should be gently poured, a bit at a time, over a few crystals of sodium acetate placed in the middle of a large petri dish. As the supersaturated sodium acetate solution touches these crystals, crystallisation should begin and the liquid will crystallise completely, giving off heat as it does so. The crystallisation can be carried out on an overhead projector to make it more visible.

What can go wrong?

Sometimes, the solution will not start to crystallise when it comes into contact with the solid crystals. If this happens, just add a few more crystals.

There are now commercial versions of this crystallisation reaction available under brand names such as HotPack which are sold as a reusable hand warmer. The supersaturated solution is packaged in a plastic pouch and contains a metal disc. Flexing the disk starts the crystallisation process and as the sodium acetate crystals form considerable heat is given out. Its temperature can reach more than 40°C. The pouch can be returned to the liquid state by heating in a pan of boiling water, which dissolves the crystals and on cooling, the hand warmer is ready for use once more. These cost in the region of £5 and make a simple demonstration which can be passed round a class.

CHAPTER 4

LIFE PROCESSES

This chapter examines the characteristics of plants. It covers the extraction of DNA, capillary action, osmosis, evaporation and cooling.

DNA

DNA stands for deoxyribonucleic acid. It is a natural polymer and contains the genetic code which describes the make-up of nearly all living things.

Extraction of DNA

Although animal DNA is minute in size and invisible to the naked eye, it is possible to extract plant DNA from wheat, which can be seen much more easily. The following experiment may be carried out both in the laboratory, in which case the resulting DNA is excellent, or in a kitchen environment, where the results may not be quite as good but are still clearly visible.

Equipment required
A bag of wheat germ (natural, untoasted), available from whole-food shops ➤

Sodium chloride
Sodium citrate
Water
Ethanol
Sodium dodecyl sulphate (SDS, a detergent)
A muslin filter
A glass stirrer
Beakers
A centrifuge
Filter paper

Best results are obtained if all the solutions are cooled in a refrigerator prior to use.

Mix about 10g of wheat germ with 125ml of a mixture of 0.14M sodium chloride and 0.01M sodium citrate for 10 minutes. This should be gently stirred to break down the plant cell walls. After this time, press gently through muslin. Keep the pulp. Repeat this extraction again.

Stir the pulp gently with 125ml of 0.2M sodium chloride and 11ml of a detergent solution, made up of SDS (5% weight by volume) in 49% ethanol, for 20 minutes. The detergent extracts the DNA into solution. Add 6.5g of solid sodium chloride, stir the mixture for 10 minutes and finally spin at about 12,000 rpm for 20 minutes in a centrifuge (refrigerated, if possible). This separates the DNA solution from the cell walls, etc. Keep the viscous supernatant.

In a large beaker, for every 100ml of supernatant collected, add 300ml of ethanol and stir with a glass rod. DNA is insoluble in alcohol. A jelly-like fibrous precipitate of DNA should form as the alcohol is added. The fibres of DNA can be collected by turning the rod in the solution. Remove the surplus ethanol by pressing the DNA between filter paper. Wash the fibres gently with 96% ethanol and again dry them with filter paper. DNA will last longer if it is kept in ethanol, inside a sealed glass tube. The fibres can be studied under a microscope but are visible to the naked eye.

It is also possible to prepare plant DNA in the kitchen using the following items.

Equipment required
Salt
A large glass containing 250ml water
10g wheat germ
Lemon juice
A tea strainer
Washing-up liquid
Vodka or gin (or similar)

Lemon juice is used as a substitute for citric acid, a tea strainer to separate the liquid containing the dissolved DNA from the broken cell wall fragments, washing-up liquid instead of pure SDS and a spirit such as vodka or gin instead of ethanol. Much less DNA is collected and the fibres are not as clearly defined. The centrifugation can be substituted by simply allowing time for the solid and liquid parts of the solution to separate out by gravity. Again, liquids should be kept in the refrigerator and for best results quantities and timings should be experimented with.

As a rough guide, start with 250ml of water in which 2 teaspoons of salt have been dissolved, and chill the liquid in the fridge. Mix half of this in a large glass with about 10g of wheat germ and add two teaspoons of lemon juice. This should be stirred and left in the fridge for about 10–15 minutes. This first stage is to break down the cell walls. The mixture should be sieved in the tea strainer or separated by gravity and the liquid decanted off and discarded. Stir the cell pulp gently with the other half of the salt solution and this time add a few drops of washing-up liquid (dissolved in a couple of teaspoons of alcohol, such as vodka). This stage extracts the DNA into solution. Stir occasionally for 15–20 minutes. Next add about 3 teaspoons of salt and stir for about 10 minutes.

Then pour off as much of the liquid as you can and keep it. Sieve the mix through a tea strainer and put all the liquid into a glass container.

Finally, add about three times as much alcohol to your liquid as you have liquid, ie if you end up with 100ml of liquid, add 300ml of alcohol. At this stage, fine white threads of DNA should become visible as the alcohol precipitates the protein out of solution. It is probably best to start with reduced quantities until the timing and amounts have been experimented with. The DNA threads can be lifted carefully out of solution and looked at under a microscope.

All of the solutions used are safe and may be flushed with water and disposed of down a sink. However, pure alcohol is inflammable and should not be allowed to come into contact with the eyes or skin.

What can go wrong?

If the initial extraction phase is not long enough, or the concentrations of sodium chloride/sodium citrate are completely wrong, then the cell walls may not be broken down and the yield of DNA may be low. If, on the other hand, the conditions are too harsh, the DNA may be broken down into tiny pieces and the results will be disappointing. If a centrifuge is available then the results will be better but if not the extraction is still possible if care is taken. The solutions should be left for sufficient time to achieve a separation between the solid cell walls and the DNA in detergent. The liquid from the pulp can then be carefully poured off.

DNA Mutations

The objective of this simple demonstration is to show by analogy the triplet code of DNA and how mutations can affect it.

Equipment required
A blackboard and chalk (or an overhead projector could be used)

Write the following sentence on the board or overhead projector:

THE OLD RED DOG WAS TOO BIG FOR HIS BED.

Each word consists of three letters like the triplet code of DNA. If a mutation were to cause a deletion of the D of OLD, the sentence would now read:

THE OLR EDD OGW AST OOB IGF ORH ISB ED.

Obviously, this is nonsense. If it were a DNA molecule, the resulting protein would probably be ineffective. If the mutation caused an inversion of the word DOG, however, the sentence would now read:

THE OLD RED GOD WAS TOO BIG FOR HIS BED.

In this case, the sentence still makes sense, but the meaning is completely changed. A protein resulting from such a mutation would have a different amino acid in one position of its sequence which could have profound implications for the way in which it worked. Such a mutation could start the formation of a tumour, cause a loss of an enzyme or another vital protein. This analogy could be extended by making other mutations, such as reversing the sentence, inserting a new word or letter, substituting a different word somewhere along the chain, etc. Simple changes in DNA can cause profound changes in the proteins made from that DNA and lead to serious changes in the biochemistry of the body.

PLANTS AND THEIR PROPERTIES

Indicators from Plants

The following list of plants can be used to prepare indicator solutions, which can be used to test the pH of many household liquids:

- red cabbage
- red onions
- blackberry
- red grapes
- radishes
- red cherries

Demonstrations and Experiments in Science

- rose petals.

The indicator solutions can be used to test the pH of liquids such as:

- vinegar
- lemon juice
- bleach
- shampoo (diluted with water)
- milk of magnesia tablets dissolved in water
- fizzy drinks
- baking soda in water
- ammonia solution.

A typical recipe is outlined below.

Equipment required
200g plant material
A blender
200ml distilled water or pure ethanol
A fine sieve (a piece of muslin or a cotton handkerchief)

Chop about 200g of plant material, such as red cabbage, and place in a blender. Add enough distilled water to cover it (about 200ml should be sufficient). The mix should be blended until completely chopped. The mixture should then be strained through a fine sieve. The chopping will have released a chemical pigment in the cells whose colour is sensitive to the pH of its solution. If particles are still present, the liquid can be allowed to settle with time and then decanted. This makes the basic indicator solution. Its colour will differ depending on the plant used.

Ethanol may also be used to extract the indicators instead of water and will give a less cloudy solution. This makes it easier to see the colour changes during use but an electric blender should not be used with ethanol since sparks may ignite the vapour.

Testing procedure

About 5–10ml (1–2 teaspoons) of indicator is needed per 100ml of test solution. The colour changes should be observed and recorded and can be compared between test solutions to give an idea of the relative acidity/alkalinity of the test liquids. The following colour changes may be observed.

Indicator source	Acid (pH=1–4)	Neutral (pH=5–8)	Alkaline (pH=9–12)
red cabbage	red/violet	green/blue	yellow/green
blackberry juice	red	violet/red	violet/blue
radishes	pale pink	clear	violet/green
red cherries	red/brown		green/brown
red onions	pink	pale green	yellow/green
red grapes	red	violet	blue

Some of these plant materials make better indicators than others since some will only change colour over a narrow range of pH values, whilst others require large changes in pH to change colour only slightly. It is also possible to make indicator paper by soaking a piece of filter paper or cloth in the indictor solution and then letting it dry. This can then be used at a later date.

Most of the extracts contain a chemical group called anthocyanins or anthoxanthins which are water soluble, natural pigments. Their chemical structure, and hence colour, depends on the pH of their surroundings but they are not ideal indicators since their colour changes are not always reversible.

The indicators themselves are safe but care must be taken with ethanol (inflammable and hazardous) and the various test solutions such as bleach, vinegar and ammonia. These can all be disposed of down the sink after dilution with large quantities of water. As stated above, ethanol or other inflammable solvents should not be used in electrical equipment such as blenders which may produce sparks.

Demonstrations and Experiments in Science

Taking Photographs Using Photosynthesis

This demonstration shows how light generates starch inside the leaves of a plant as a result of photosynthesis and uses this fact to create a photograph on a leaf.

Equipment required
A non-variegated geranium plant with large undamaged leaves
A slide projector with a powerful bulb and slides with a simple, clear picture
Ethanol
A shallow dish which is large enough for the leaf to fit in
2 glass or thin clear plastic plates
Iodine solution
Beakers
Elastic bands

Place the plant in the dark for at least 48 hours before the demonstration is due to take place. This should remove most of the starch from the leaves. In a darkened laboratory, break a leaf off and place between two glass or clear plastic plates, so that it is sandwiched flat, and secure with elastic bands. Set up the sandwiched leaf so that the slide can be projected onto it (this is best checked in advance, taking care to get the focusing correct). Then project the image onto the leaf for about one hour. For best results use a clear, simple image with strong contrast (a black and white image is best for this purpose).

Next, remove the leaf from between the plates and place in a beaker of boiling ethanol. The leaf should gradually lose its green colour as the chlorophyll is removed from the cells. A change of ethanol may be required. When most of the leaf's colour has gone, remove and dry it carefully. Place it in a shallow dish and drop iodine solution onto it and the slide picture should emerge as the iodine reacts with the starch formed by light in the leaf. Wash off any excess iodine solution. The image on the leaf should be a very good version of the slide. Images can be improved by changing the timing of the slide illumination. If the leaf is not too dark green, the stage involving boiling ethanol can be missed out but the final image will not be so clear.

What can go wrong?
Care must be taken to keep light away from the leaf once it is picked from the plant. Apparatus such as the slide projector and the boiling ethanol should be set up beforehand so that the leaf has little chance of receiving illumination from room lights, etc. The ethanol should be heated on a water bath in a fume cupboard. The leaf will become very delicate after boiling and will tear easily so it must be handled gently.

OSMOSIS

Osmosis is the process which moves water across a semi-permeable membrane from a region of high water concentration to one of lower water concentration. Larger molecules such as sugars are unable to move through the small pores in a semi-permeable membrane.

Osmosis Through a Semi-Permeable Membrane

The effect of osmosis may be demonstrated using the membrane around an egg.

Equipment required
500ml of vinegar or acetic acid
3 fresh chicken eggs
3 400ml beakers
Sugar or treacle
A strong dye such as methylene blue or food colour, dissolved in some water
Scales

A fresh egg is placed in a beaker, covered with vinegar and left to stand for up to two days. During this time, the acetic acid in the vinegar dissolves the calcium carbonate egg shell, liberating carbon dioxide and water and leaving the egg yolk and white contained inside an outer membrane. If left in vinegar after the shell has dissolved, this exposed membrane will start to swell up. It should be removed from the vinegar as soon as the shell has been dissolved. The exposed membrane containing the egg white and yolk may then be used to demonstrate the effects of osmosis. The egg should be carefully removed from the beaker, washed gently in water and patted dry. Three eggs should be prepared in this way.

One should be placed gently in a beaker containing plain water (egg A). Another (egg B) should be placed in a beaker containing a dye dissolved in water and the third (egg C) should be placed in a solution of sugar in water (about 100g of sugar dissolved in 400ml of water should be sufficient) or a mixture of 75% treacle and 25% water. Eggs A and C should be weighed every hour or two. Egg A should be observed to swell and to gain weight as the water moves through the membrane into the egg, whilst the opposite effect should be seen with egg C. The concentrated sugar solution around egg C will draw the water out of egg C through its membrane whilst the sugar molecules are too large to move through the membrane. Changes in weight may be fairly small and may change by as little as 1% every hour. These changes may be plotted over time. Egg B may be taken out of the water/dye solution after 24 hours and washed carefully. The dye should have moved inside the egg, which will have become swollen. If egg B is now placed in the sugar or treacle solution, over a period of many hours the colouring present inside will move by osmosis from the inside of the egg to the external solution.

What can go wrong?

The most common mistake is breaking or tearing the egg membrane while they are being weighed. As egg A absorbs extra water, it will become slightly distended and more likely to tear. Errors in weighing will affect the results, so care must be taken to properly dry the eggs each time they are weighed. Changes in weight of only a few percent occur over a period of hours so weighing must be accurate.

A similar demonstration to that described above may be carried out using sausage casing, bought from a butchers shop. This casing should be natural, ie made from the intestines of cows or pigs (which is a semi-permeable membrane like the membrane around the egg).

Equipment required
Sausage casings (a few metres will be enough)
String or cotton
5–10 beakers depending on the number of experiments to be carried out
Sugar
Food dye
Water

The sausage casing is cut into short lengths of about five inches and one end should be tied tightly with string or cotton. The sausage skin can be filled with either water with food dye added or a concentrated sugar solution. Whichever is used, the other should be placed in the beaker around it and the sausage case should be sealed at the other end, again by tying with string or cotton. If the skin is filled with sugar solution, it should not be tied so that the skin is taut but so that the 'sausage' is fairly floppy. On the other hand, if it is filled with water/food dye, it should be tied tightly so the sausage is rigid.

When the sausages are placed in the beakers and left for a period of hours, it will be seen that the water will move from the concentrated side to the dilute side (ie into the concentrated sugar solution) and the food dye will move with it. The osmosis can be monitored by measuring changes in weight or, less accurately, by changes in tension of the sausage casing.

CAPILLARY ACTION

Capillary action is a phenomenon which plays a vital role in many areas of biology. It describes a force which 'pulls' liquids along very fine tubes or capillaries and plays an important role in the way plants and trees draw up water from the soil to their leaves. It results from the sum of the surface tension and adhesion forces which occur at a liquid/solid/gas interface inside a narrow space, such as that inside capillary tubing or inside xylem tissue in plants.

Plant Conductive Tissue

Plants carry water through their stems to their leaves. Stems also carry nutrients from the roots to the leaves. This can be illustrated by the following demonstration.

Equipment required
Food colouring
2 beakers, half filled with water
A knife
A large piece of celery with leaves on top
A magnifying glass

The beakers should be about half full of water. Add red food colouring to one beaker of water and blue to the other. Take one stalk of celery with leaves and split it from the bottom up about half way. Using a good magnifying glass, the celery stalk should be examined and the string like bundles which carry fluid to the leaves found. The beakers should be placed side by side. Put the ends of the celery in the beakers so that one side of the stalk is in red food colouring solution and the other half is in blue food colouring solution. Over a period from a few hours up to a day, the leaves of the celery should change colour as the coloured water travels up the capillaries in the stem. When the leaves have changed colour, a piece of stalk can then be sliced through and the deep stains on the

Life Processes

conducting tissue become obvious. The pipe like strings or bundles are the nutrient carrying tubes.

Use a microscope to further examine the tissue. Cut a thin cross-section and examine the tissue under low magnification. You can actually see the nutrient-carrying tubes or xylem. Try colouring celery a variety of colours. By watering potted plants with various coloured dyes you can record what happens to the flowers, leaves and stems. Would the leaves of germinating seeds (beans) be coloured if the water source contained dye? Place freshly cut white flowers in dye and watch the colour change. Pupils can observe in the detailed structure in flower petals as the dye colours the conducting tissue.

Glass Plates

Capillary action may also be shown using the following demonstration.

Equipment required
2 glass plates (30cm×15cm)
A piece of thread
A shallow tank
Water coloured with food dye

The two glass plates are clamped together along one vertical edge and separated at the opposite edge by a piece of thread, placed between the plates. The plates should then be placed in the tank and supported so that they are stable. Water, with food dye added for clarity, should then be poured carefully into the tank. Water will be drawn by capillary action up the edge at which the glass plates are touching. The water level should form a hyperbola, with the highest point occurring where the plates touch and the lowest point at the opposite side of the plates at water level. The height of the water rise should be inversely proportional to the plate separation. This is shown in figure 16 on page 98. The angle between the plates is exaggerated for clarity in the diagram.

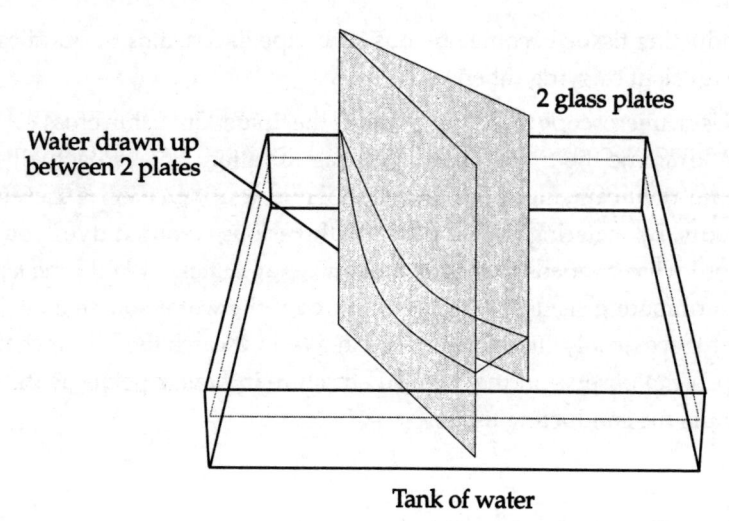

Figure 16

What can go wrong?
The plates should be sufficiently stable so that they will not fall over and need only be 30cm square at the largest. No hyperbola surface will be observed if the angle at which the plates meet is too large, since the air gap between the plates will be too great to allow capillary action to occur. The angle at which the plates touch should therefore be varied to find the best demonstration of the effect. This can be done by using different thicknesses of thread or wire to separate the plates.

OTHER PROCESSES

Liquid Polarity and Surface Tension

The behaviour of liquids at an interface is vital for life. Almost all biochemical reactions in living creatures occur at an interface, formed either between a solid and a liquid or a liquid and a gas. The surface tension properties of a liquid are thus very important. The surface of a liquid has some similarity to a stretched elastic sheet. Placing a small object, such as a needle, onto the surface of water will result in the needle sitting in a small depression on the water's surface as if it were sitting on an elastic sheet. Surface tension is actually a force which arises from the tendency of a liquid surface to contract. The origin of the force may be explained by considering the difference between water molecules at the surface and those in the middle of the liquid far away from any surface. The latter will be surrounded by other water molecules while those at the surface will be only partially enclosed. It is this imbalance which gives rise to a force which acts along the surface of a liquid.

The effect of surface tension may be shown as follows.

Equipment required
A shallow dish filled with water
A needle or razor blade
Detergent

Fill a shallow dish with water and place a needle gently on the surface. It will 'float'. Similarly, a razor blade will also be supported by surface tension. Then add a few drops of detergent to the water and after several seconds the needle and the razor blade should sink. The needle and the razor blade are made of metal and, metal being more dense than water, should sink. However, they are supported because of the strength of the attractive forces between the water molecules on the surface. The detergent acts by coming between the water molecules and breaking their attractive forces. The force on the floating object applied by gravity is then sufficient to push the water molecules apart and the needle and the razor blade will sink.

What can go wrong?

The presence of traces of soap or detergent in a beaker will prevent the floating of a needle or razor. The glassware and the water should therefore be very clean. It may be easier to float the metal objects if they have a thin coating of grease, which could be obtained by rubbing between fingers. They should also be completely dry before being put onto the water surface.

Demonstrations and Experiments in Science

Forces between molecules can be shown using the following demonstration.

Equipment required
A shallow dish filled with water
Lycopodium powder
Mineral oil
Olive oil
An overhead projector

The lycopodium powder is sprinkled over the surface of the water where it forms a thin layer. A drop of mineral oil is placed onto the surface and stays as a tiny oil bead. By contrast, if a drop of olive oil is placed on the surface, it rapidly spreads out, pushing the lycopodium powder in front of it.

These different effects arise from the different intermolecular forces which are occurring. Water is a polar liquid since its structure gives it a small but finite charge. On the other hand, mineral oil is a non-polar liquid, composed entirely of hydrogen and carbon molecules. For this reason, it repels (and is repelled by) water and is thus termed hydrophobic. When a drop of mineral oil is added to the surface of water, it tries to minimise its surface contact with the water and beads up into a small droplet. Olive oil, on the other hand, has a different chemical structure to mineral oil. It is made of molecules which contain 'ester' groups, which have a slight charge and are thus attracted to water. When a drop is added to the surface of the water, the olive oil spreads out to maximise its interaction with the water and it forms a sheet only one molecule thick (a monolayer). The lycopodium powder is used to show this spreading effect clearly. This demonstration can be carried out very effectively on an overhead projector.

The effect of the meniscus on floating objects can be shown using two or three small pieces of wood or paraffin floating in a large crystallising dish of water. If the dish is not full, they will cling to the sides but if more water is added so that the meniscus rises above the dish, the floating objects will leave the edge and assemble in the middle of the water surface.

Evaporation and Cooling

A bottle of milk can be cooled efficiently by wrapping it in wet cloth and then standing this in a bucket of cold water. If the rate of evaporation can be speeded up by placing the wrapped up bottle in a draught, then the cooling will be more efficient. Humans, animals and plants keep cool by evaporating water from their surfaces and this type of cooling is vital for maintaining temperatures at a constant level.

If a little methylated spirits or eau-de-Cologne is spilt onto the hand, it will evaporate immediately and the skin will feel very cold. This is because these liquids have low boiling points and change from liquid to vapour quite easily at ordinary temperatures. The reason for the temperature change is that evaporation requires latent heat, which is obtained from the skin in the above example. The heat required is called the latent heat of evaporation. Some liquids are particularly useful for demonstrating the cooling effect. A simple experiment is to compare the temperature of a bottle of cold water which has been wrapped in a wet rag for a few hours, with one that has not. Alternatively, the feeling of acetone or methylated spirits on the skin will show the cooling effect, although the temperature changes will be small.

A more impressive example of cooling by evaporation is outlined below.

Equipment required
A 250ml beaker
200ml of ether
A block of wood
Some water
A pair of bellows or an air pump
A thermometer

The ether is poured into the beaker, which should be placed on top of the wooden block. A small pool of water should be made on the block first so that the base of the beaker is wet. The beaker and block are placed in a fume cupboard and a tube from the bellows or air pump is placed in the ether. When air is passed through the ether, the volatile liquid will begin to evaporate in the stream of air. The vapour is carried away as the bubbles of air rise to the surface. This increases the rate of evaporation to such an extent that the liquid ether will cool rapidly. As the latent heat of evaporation is coming directly from the ether itself, the liquid will soon cool to below 0°C. Heat will be extracted from the beaker itself, and then from the water around the base of the beaker. Eventually, the water around the base of the beaker will freeze. This cooling can be monitored by placing a thermometer in the ether every few minutes. Alternatively, the temperature of the ether can be monitored continuously using a simple thermocouple attached to a chart recorder or an electronic thermometer.

Ether is highly flammable and should not be inhaled. This experiment should be carried out in a fume cupboard away from naked flames.

An alternative procedure for showing the endothermic nature of evaporation is given below.

Equipment required

500ml acetone

A thick walled 1 litre round-bottomed flask

A glass thermometer or thermocouple thermometer

A three-way glass tap

Thick walled rubber tubing

A water aspirator

A rubber bung with 2 holes, one to hold a short piece of glass tubing and the other for the thermometer or thermocouple (they should be a tight fit)

The acetone is placed in the flask. The thermometer or thermocouple is inserted through one hole in the bung so that it will be below the level of the acetone. A short piece of glass tube with a three-way tap attached is inserted through the other hole, and the bung pushed into the neck of the flask. The water aspirator is connected to a water tap and attached to one arm of the three-way tap. The flask should be placed behind a safety screen since there is a possibility that it could implode during the demonstration. Both the thermometer and the glass tube should fit tightly into the bung since the aspirator is used to suck the air out of the flask. To begin with, the initial temperature of the acetone should be read off. Then the aspirator should be used to suck the air out of the flask. This reduces the pressure in the flask and when it is low enough it will cause the acetone to begin to boil. (Its boiling point is reduced at low pressure, as with water.) As the acetone boils and evaporates its temperature will fall rapidly, and this temperature drop may be read on the thermometer. Moisture may condense on the outside of the flask. Afterwards, the three-way tap may be turned slowly to readmit air into the flask.

Since acetone is flammable, the experiment should be carried out away from naked flames and the aspirator should be placed on a tap in the fume cupboard so that acetone vapour is drawn away. As mentioned above, a safety screen should be used around the flask.

What can go wrong?

Great care must be taken when inserting glassware through rubber or cork bungs. Teachers should wear gloves and use a lubricant such as washing-up liquid. The most obvious problem is an air leak around the bung which will prevent the air being sucked out of the flask. This should be checked for if the acetone does not start to boil. Acetone temperatures of between 5–10°C should be achievable with this set-up.

Bioluminescence in Nature

There are a number of living creatures around the world which give out light as a way of attracting either prey or mates. These include glow-worms (which may be found in Britain), fireflies, fish, algae and fungi. Some of these creatures use a chemical reaction involving luciferase and ATP. These reactions may be simulated using either the chemiluminescent reactions described on page 46 or with the use of light sticks, which can be purchased from Miltrain Ltd (see page 120 for contact details).

CHAPTER 5

COMPUTERS AND THE INTERNET

BUILD YOUR OWN DISPLAYS

The power of multimedia computers can be used to put together custom-designed presentations or displays in order to enhance lessons and to display material. Although this can prove very time consuming, by using one of the powerful presentation packages available the results can be extremely worthwhile educationally and look highly professional. This approach means that a teacher can tailor the display precisely to the requirements of his or her pupils. It is possible to include sound and video clips, pictures and text into a package which can be run continually in a loop or used interactively. Listed below are some programs which may be used to construct presentations. They are available either in IBM-compatible or Apple Macintosh formats.

Powerpoint

This presentation package can be used to generate overheads, slides or handouts and can also be used to combine a series of images and texts into a presentation. Thanks to the presence of helpful guides, it is quite an easy package to use and a satisfactory presentation can be put together in quite a short time. Pictures, graphs, etc can be imported from other programs and incorporated into the presentation package.

Multimedia Toolbook

Asymetrix Multimedia Toolbook is a 'visual authoring system' which can be used to build interactive presentations or self-running demonstrations in Windows. It involves the use of a relatively simple scripting language which allows you to build a variety of presentation styles. This makes this package more versatile than Powerpoint but also more complicated to use.

Mathematica

Mathematica is a powerful mathematical software package created by Wolfram Research Inc which is increasingly finding applications in teaching both at university level and in secondary schools. It features a number of packages which can either be linked together with other programs, such as spreadsheets, or used alone. Packages available include those for plotting the propagation of sound waves, plotting world maps, plotting molecular structure and molecular motions and the positions of the planets and stars. More information is available from the Wolfram homepage at http://www.wri.com/ or from the journal *Mathematica in Education*, published quarterly by TELOS/Springer-Verlag. Demonstration discs are available in IBM-compatible or Apple Macintosh formats from Wolfram. There is a Mathematica bulletin board which provides resources for teachers which can be accessed via modem on +1 708 956 5344.

INFORMATION VIA THE INTERNET

The Internet is a useful source for information on demonstrations. The sites detailed below are just a small selection of those available. There are more sites are appearing all the time, although most are US sites and are written predominantly for a US audience and teaching style. These sites can be avoided by using a search engine which allows searches to be made in specific regions of the world, eg HotBot which allows searches to be made of sites in western Europe only.

Great care should be taken when typing in addresses. They must be entered exactly as shown. There should be no spaces within the address and you should be particularly careful to check punctuation and capitalization. Where Internet addresses have been incorporated into sentences they may be followed by a full stop where they come at the end of a sentence: this does not form part of the address and should not be typed in.

Information for Schools

One page of interest to schools is the Schools Internet homepage at http://www.schools.co.uk/. It allows schools to find information on a range of topics. EduWeb allows online searches for educational resources at http://www.rmpl.co.uk/eduweb/eduweb.html.

Net Security

Net security may be provided by:

- Surfwatch, whose address is http:// www.surfwatch.com
- NetNanny at http://www.netnanny.com/netnanny
- Cyberpatrol at http://www.microsys.com/cyber.

Physics Demonstrations

The following sites have very good links to worldwide physics demonstrations:

- http://gakugei.gakugei-hs.setagaya.tokyo.jp/buturilink.html
- http://www.mip.berkeley.edu/physics/physics.html

Also recommended is a list of physics educational resources at http://www-hpcc.astro.washington.edu/scied/physics.html. Interactive Physics II is a computer package which is designed to allow physics experiments and demonstrations to be carried out via computer. It is US based and some universities and schools are putting their own demonstrations onto the Internet for others to use. Further information and pricing can be obtained by fax on +1 415 574 7541. A demonstration version of the program can be downloaded from Knowledge Revolution Inc, homepage at http://info.itp.berkeley.edu/vol1/.

Robotic Telescopes

The Automated Telescope Facility at Iowa University may be found at http://inferno.physics.uiowa.edu/. The telescope at Santa Barbara, University of California allows you to download images and programs. It has a bulletin board in the US on +1 805 893 2650 and may also be found at http://www.deepspace.ucsb.edu/rot.htm. A complete list of remote controlled telescope sites may be found at http://www.telescope.org/rti/automated.html.

Lasers and Optics

The following sites provide educational information on lasers and their uses:

- http://www.laserfantasy.com/lasers.html
- http://www.splasers.com
- http://www.holoworld.com/
- http://www.best.com/~lasrus/rlaser.html
- http://www.ieee.org/newtech/reports/leo/report.html
- http://www.scimedia.com/chem-ed/optics/sources/lasers.htm

In addition, the Microsoft Encarta encyclopaedia has a good section describing lasers, including an animated sequence showing how lasers work.

Biology Demonstrations

Quick demonstrations in biology may be found at http://nesen.unl.edu/methods/biodemo.html. There is an educational resource list for teachers available at http://www.esu.edu/~bbq/ed_resources.html. Animated teaching software, including physiology demonstrations may be downloaded from http://www.neoucom.edu/DEPTS/NEUR/WEB/animation/animation.html.

The US Activities Exchange site has a wide variety of biological and life science demonstrations and experiments, though it is tailored for teaching in the US. It can be accessed at http://www.gene.com/ae/AE/AEC/AEF/1996/. At the Field Museum of Natural History in Chicago web site there are some simple activities for younger children, such as a prehistoric crossword and quiz, flickbooks that show how dinosaurs walked and an activity to show the relative sizes of dinosaurs. This site is at http://www.vol.it/mirror/field/museum/education/LOTguide4.html.

Dissection on the Internet

Various stages of a frog dissection, including detailed images, can be seen at http://george.lbl.gov/ITG.hm.pg.docs/Whole.Frog/. A detailed description of a dissection of a cow's eye can be found at http://www.exploratorium.edu//learning_studio/cow_eye/index.html. This includes tips on how to carry out the dissection, a description of how the eye works and other useful pointers.

Volcanoes

Details of why and how volcanoes erupt can be found at http://volcano.und.nodak.edu/. This user-friendly site has updates on recent eruptions around the world.

Sound Demonstrations

A multimedia presentation describing sound and auditory perception can be found at http://www.music.mcgill.ca/auditory/Auditory.html. It illustrates some principles of our understanding of the sound world about us. This includes auditory demonstrations, discussion and experiments as well as a history of the subject. To get maximum benefit from this site a sound card is recommended.

Chemistry Demonstrations

An interactive periodic table may be found at http://mwanal.lanl.gov/julie/imagemap/periodic/periodic.html. The Imperial College London Chemistry department has good links from its homepage at http://www.ch.ic.ac.uk.

Other chemistry demonstrations or links may be found at http://wharton.stark.k12.oh.us/staffwebpages/chiudioni/. The *Journal of Chemical Education* online site features many demonstrations and experiments that may be useful at http://jchemed.chem.wisc.edu/.

Molecular modelling is a way of visualising molecular structure on computer and is becoming an increasingly powerful research tool for studying chemicals and drugs. Information on molecular modelling may be found at http://www.nyu.edu/pages/mathmol/quick_tour.html.

Ask an Expert

There are a number of sites in the US where experts in particular fields may be contacted and answers provided to questions posed by e-mail. The journal *Scientific American* has one ask an expert site at http://www.sciam.com/askexpert/index.html. Another such site designed for US schools may be found at http://www.sol.com.sg/classroom/ask.html. An ask an astronaut site is available at http://shuttle.nasa.gov/sts-69/crew/question.html.

CHAPTER 6

SAFETY ISSUES

Many chemicals are hazardous to the skin, eyes or lungs and great care should be taken in handling them. Similarly, care should be exercised in their disposal. If in doubt, check with your local safety officer. Croner's *Manual for Heads of Science* contains detailed information regarding the hazards, storage and use of chemicals.

Electrical safety is also extremely important and can be a major source of danger. For example, in lasers the power source should be treated with the same, if not more, care than the laser light itself.

The publishers cannot accept responsibility for any mishaps or accidents arising from these demonstrations or experiments since supervison in the classroom is the responsibility of the teacher in charge.

LASER SAFETY

It is recommended that the sources of information on page 113 are consulted before using lasers in the classroom. Below are some of the most important points to bear in mind.

Lasers are classified according to their ability to damage eyes or skin. They are grouped into five categories, ranging from class 1 to 4. In most cases, only class 1 and 2 lasers will be encountered in the school environment. All laser devices should be clearly labelled by their manufacturer with their safety classification and this should be checked before use. Class 1 lasers are totally enclosed systems and thus are inherently safe since normally there is no access to the laser beam itself. However, their use in teaching is limited. Semiconductor lasers built for compact disc players or telecommunications devices are usually in this class. Class 2 lasers are low power lasers whose output power is limited to below 1mW. Although some eye protection is provided by the blink response, staring into the beam may eventually result in eye damage. Class 3A lasers are medium power lasers which should probably not be used in schools. Class 3B and 4 lasers are medium to high power lasers which should not be used in schools at all.

Before use, sufficient time must be taken by teachers to acquaint themselves with any demonstrations or experiments so that they know where the laser beams are travelling and from where they can be safely viewed by the pupils. Demonstrations should not be placed at eye level and any stray beams or reflections must be checked for and blocked as near to their source as possible. Teachers should also ensure that all optical components (laser, lenses, mirrors, etc) are stable and firmly mounted since unpredicted motion may aim the laser beam at pupils. Laser warning signs should also be displayed outside the classroom. It would be wise to explicitly instruct pupils not to look into the laser beam.

Despite the recommendations in the early Department of Education and Science memos, it is generally accepted that the use of laser goggles is unnecessary since they are expensive, cumbersome and can make it harder for a demonstrator to see stray reflections or beams. One way of ensuring simple and safe operation is to build the demonstration onto a rigid base board, with exposed laser beams enclosed in clear plastic tubes as far as is possible and all components firmly fixed to the board. Ideally, the laser itself should be key operated to prevent unauthorised use.

Some lasers, for example helium/neon lasers, use a high voltage source which could represent a potential danger. Since most new semiconductor lasers rely on a low voltage battery supply, they are safer in this respect. Although the precautions above seem daunting, the use of a low voltage class 2 diode laser in a classroom environment is as safe as most other science experiments.

USEFUL PUBLICATIONS

Association for Science Education, *Safeguards in the School Laboratory*. 10th Edition, 1996.

British Standard BS 4803, *Radiation Safety of Laser Products and Systems*. Part 2, 1983.

British Standard BS EN 60825, *Radiation Safety of Laser Products*. 1992.

CLEAPSS, *CLEAPSS Laboratory Handbook*. School Science Service, Brunel University, 1996.

DES Administrative Memorandum 7/70, *Uses of Lasers in Schools*.

DFEE, *Safety in Science Education*. HMSO, 1996.

Muir, G D (ed), *Hazards in the Chemical Laboratory*. The Chemical Society, 1977.

Scottish Office Education Department Circular 7/95, *Uses of Lasers in Laboratory Work*.

FURTHER INFORMATION

There are a number of other useful sources of information and resources, some of which are described below. In addition, there are a growing number of theatre groups who present science through interactive drama.

SCIENCE QUESTIONS

Science Line is a public science enquiry service which can provide answers to scientific questions. Run by Broadcasting Support Services, it is funded by the Royal Society and the Wellcome Trust, amongst others. As well as giving access to scientists on the other end of a phone line it has links to over 1000 experts all over the UK. It may be contacted by e-mail at: sci.net@campus.bt.com or by phone on 0345 600 444. There is also a web site which features many of the questions that have been posed over the years. This may be found at http://www.campus.bt.com/Campus World/pub/ScienceNet/.

Talking Science+ is an enquiry service providing contact with lecturers and speakers in local regions who are prepared to give talks to non-specialist audiences. They can be contacted on 0171-287 0980.

DRAMA AND EXHIBITIONS

Science Alive uses interactive educational drama to convey scientific concepts through characterisation and experiments in which the audience can take part. Science Alive is run by Phillip Reader, who can be contacted at 22 Ashview Gardens, Ashford, Middlesex, TW15 3RD (tel: 01784 889671).

Floating Point Science Theatre perform live in schools and incorporate mime, theatre and audience participation in their presentations. Their touring schedule for 1996/97 includes most of the UK and they can be contacted at the Widmore Centre, Nightingale Lane, Bromley, Kent, BR1 2SG (tel: 0181-313 3832; fax: 0181-313 3843).

School Works is a travelling hands-on science exhibition which is operated by Science Projects, an educational charity. Its exhibits on materials include demonstrations of surfaces, appropriate materials, compressible materials, viscosity, strength and atoms. Other subjects covered include energy, light, sound, life and forces. Key stages 1 to 3 are addressed and teacher's notes are supplied with curriculum links and ideas for further activities. School Works can be contacted at 20 St James Street, Hammersmith, London W6 9RW (tel: 0181-741 7437).

UNIVERSITIES AND COLLEGES

Local universities and colleges often run informal schemes offering lecturers to schools free of charge. This is a much under-used resource and offers advantages not just to schools, who can obtain high quality lecturers and demonstrations, but also gives the lecturers an opportunity to broaden their teaching skills and to advertise their instituitions to the next generation of college students. Contact should be made via the Press Office, Schools Liaison Office or directly to the department of interest.

Alternatively, the Institute of Biology, the Institute of Physics and the Royal Society of Chemistry can be contacted and they can put interested parties in touch with lecturers. The Royal Institution can also be contacted for advice.

Addresses

Institute of Biology
20–22 Queensberry Place
London SW7 2DZ
Tel: 0171-581 8333

Institute of Physics
76 Portland Place
London W1N 4AA
Tel: 0171-470 4800

The Royal Institution
21 Albermarle Street
London W1X 4BS
Tel: 0171-409 2992

Royal Society of Chemistry
Burlington House
Piccadilly
London W1V OBN
Tel: 0171-437 8656

USEFUL PUBLICATIONS

Demonstrations and Experiments

There are numerous publications describing demonstrations and experiments but many are out of print or hard to get hold of. Very good source material may be found in the *Journal of Chemical Education*, published by the American Chemical Society, and in the *School Science Review*, published by the Association for Science Education.

Faraday, M, *The Chemical History of a Candle*.
This classic text may be hard to find, but it represents the classic demonstration lecture. It uses a simple piece of chemistry, the burning candle, to illustrate a wide variety of chemical principles and has a lot to offer in terms of clarity and simplicity.

Iddon, B, *The Magic of Chemistry*. BDH Publications, 1985.
A very practical guide to chemistry demonstrations, this short book covers a number of the most interesting areas of chemical demonstrations.

Lister, T, *Classic Chemical Demonstrations*. The Royal Society of Chemistry, 1996.
This book contains an excellent selection of chemistry demonstrations and experiments put together with much consideration for the practical aspects of teaching.

Shakhashiri, B Z, *Chemical Demonstrations: A Handbook for Teachers of Chemistry*. The University of Wisconsin Press, 1985.
This is a huge dictionary of chemistry demonstrations, in four volumes with detailed discussion sections for each demonstration.

Taylor, C, *The Art and Science of Demonstration Lectures*. Academic Press, 1983.
Dealing with more than just the demonstrations themselves, this book make fascinating reading.

Lasers and Light

Billings, C, *Lasers: The New Technology of Light*. Facts on File Science Source Books, Facts on File Inc, New York, 1992.

Griffiths, J, *Lasers and Holograms*. Exploration and Discovery Series, McMillan.

Hecht, J, *Making Light Work*. Inside Science Series, *New Scientist*, 17 June 1989.

Hecht, J, *Understanding Lasers*. Howard Sams and Co, Indiana, 1988.

Kerrod, R, *Light and Lasers*. Insights Series, Oxford University Press, 1993.

Mace, W K, *Manual for School Laser Demonstrations*. Philip Harris Science Publishers, 1983.

McLaren, P, *Laser Experiments Manual*. Griffin (gives details of experiments and background notes).

Myring, L, and Kimmitt, M, *Lasers*. Usbourne Publishing, 1991.

Pearson, R L, *"Laser Listener"* in *Radio-Electronics*, October 1987.

SUPPLIERS

Suppliers of Lasers, Optics and Other Equipment

Edmund Scientific (distributed by Ealing Scientific)
Greychaine Road
Watford
Herts WD2 4PW
Tel: 01923 242261
Free catalogue available. Excellent selection of cheap and more expensive lasers and a wide variety of optics.

Esoteric Lasertech
180 Ifield Road
London SW10 9AF
Tel: 0370 392801
Very cheap source of diode lasers and laser-related equipment.

Fisons Scientific UK Ltd
Bishop Meadow Road
Loughborough
Leicestershire LE11 5RG
Tel: 01509 231166
Demonstration equipment suppliers.

Philip Harris Scientific
618 Western Avenue

Park Royal
London W3 0TE
Tel: 0181-992 5555
Suppliers of general demonstration equipment and optics.

Maplin Electronics
Numerous trade centres in UK (see *Yellow Pages*). Diode lasers and kits for helium/neon lasers available, amongst other things. Catalogues on sale in larger newsagents.

RS Electronics Components Ltd
PO Box 99
Corby
Northants NN17 1RS
National order line: 01536 201201
Diode lasers and opto-electronics sections in a free three part catalogue.

Chemical Suppliers

All companies will supply free catalogues on request.

Aldrich (includes Fluka Chemicals)
The Old Brickyard
New Road
Gillingham
Dorset SP8 4JL
Tel: 0800 717181

ICI Chemicals and Polymers
PO Box 14
The Heath
Runcorn
Cheshire WA7 4QF
Tel: 01928 514444

Miltrain Ltd
The Business Centre

Further Information

3 Wansdown Place
London SW6 1DN
Tel: 0171-381 1899

Scott-Bader Co Ltd (source of polyurethane foam)
Wollaston
Wellingborough
Northants NM29 7RL
Tel: 01933 663100

Sigma Chemical Company Ltd
Fancy Road
Poole
Dorset BH17 7BR
Tel: 0800 373731

Union Carbide Chemicals (one source of polyox)
PO Box 54
Wilton
Middlesborough
Cleveland TS90 8JA
Tel: 01642 374000

INDEX

A

acetic acid 24
acetone 101, 103
alcohol 88
Aldrich 120
algae 103–4
American Chemical Society 117
American Cyanamid Company 45
ammonia 39–40
anthocyanins 91
anthoxanthins 91
appropriateness 4
aquariums 28
Arrhenius plot 46
Association for Science Education 117
astronauts, web sites 110
astronomy 24–6
　see also telescopes

Asymetrix Multimedia Toolbook 106
ATP 104

B

beam divergence 52, 54
Belousov-Zhabotinsky reaction 43–5
Betelgeuse 23
biology, web sites 109
bioluminescence 103–4
birefringence 34–7
black body radiation equation 16
black light 17
borax 79
Bradford University 25
Broadcasting Support Services 115
BS EN 60825 53–4

bubbles 30–2
bulletin boards, Mathematica 106
butyl rubber 68

C

cameras 22–3
  single lens reflex 15, 21–2
capillary action 96–8
car headlights 22
centrifuge 88
Charles' Law 72
Chemical Demonstrations (Shakhashiri) 46
chemicals
  as indicators 40–1
  safe handling 3, 111
  suppliers 120–1
chemiluminescence 45–6
  bioluminescence 104
  clock reaction 49–50
  reactions 46–9
chemistry, web sites 110
class 2 semiconductor lasers 53
clock reaction 41–3
  chemiluminescence 49–50
Coates, Bill 41
coherent light 51, 52
colleges 116–17

colour
  and light scattering 29–30
  phosphors 17
  primary 9
  sodium and neon lights 18–19
  and temperature 16, 23–4
colour change 38–51
compact discs 14–15
computers 105–6
  see also web sites
cooling 101–3
copper sulphate dust 50
crests 10, 11–12
crystallisation 82–3
Cyalume 45
Cyberpatrol 107
cysteine 50

D

demonstrations 1–5
  publications describing 117–18
deoxyribonucleic acid *see* DNA
Department of Education and Science 112
detergents 31
diffraction gratings 14–15, 20–2, 62–3
diode lasers 53–5, 60
directionality, laser light 52

discharge lamps 18–19, 22
dissection, web sites 109
DMSO (dimethylsulphoxide) 48–9
DNA 85
　extraction 85–8
　mutations 88–9
double slit experiment 60–2
dough 76
drama 2, 3, 116

E

eau-de-Cologne 101
Edmund Scientific 9, 20, 22, 60
　address 119
EduWeb 107
eggs 93–5
elastic bands 11, 71
elasticity
　liquids 77–8
　rubber 68–70
electrical safety 111
Esoteric Lasertech 119
ethanol 90, 91
ether 102
evaporation 101–3
exhibitions 116
experimental technique 3

experiments
　definition 2–3
　see also demonstrations
expert web sites 110
eye safety 55, 112

F

failure 4
Field Museum of Natural History 109
filaments 16
films (photographic) 15, 23
fireflies 103–4
fish 103–4
Fisons Scientific UK Ltd 119
flame emission spectrometry 20
flame test 19–20
Floating Point Science Theatre 2, 116
fluorescence, polymer solutions 74
fluorescent tubes 16–17
forces 66, 73
fountains 39–40
fungi 103–4

G

gallium arsenide 22
gas velocities 69
gases, solubility 39–40
geometry 32
glass plates 97–8
glass prisms 7–9, 12–13
glow-worms 103–4
glycerin 31

H

hand warmers 83
heat 23
helium/neon lasers 53, 55, 112
    beam divergence 54
    wavelength 60
holography 55
HotPack 83
hydrogen chloride 40
hydrogen peroxide 48–9, 50

I

ice 24
ice lens 38
ICI Chemicals and Polymers 79, 120

Iddon, Brian 41, 45
Imperial College 110
incandescent bulbs 16, 18–19
incoherent light 51, 52
Indian ink 29–30
indicators
    chemical 40–1
    plants 89–91
Indigo Carmine 40–1
Institute of Biology 116–17
Institute of Physics 116–17
intensity, laser light 52
Interactive Physics II 107–8
interference 30–2
    laser light 60–2
Internet *see* web sites
isoprene 68

J

Journal of Chemical Education 110, 117

K

key stage 3 66, 72–3
key stage 4 66, 72–3
kinetic theory 72
Knowledge Revolution Inc 108

Index

L

laboratory safety 3
laser light 51–2
   polarisation 32
   wavelength measurement 60–3
laser pointers 54
laser safety 111–13
lasers
   buying 52–5
   demonstrations 55–63
   publications 118–19
   web sites 108
latent heat 101
lecture experiments 2
light 51–2
   bioluminescence 103–4
   interference 30–2
   polarisation 32–8
   publications 118–19
   see also laser light; white light
Light Amplification by Stimulated Emission of Radiation *see* lasers
light bulbs 16, 18–19
light scattering 27–30
light sources 22–3
   identifying 19–22
   types 16–19
light sticks 45–6
   bioluminescence 104

liquid crystal displays 34
liquids, polarity 98, 100–1
listening devices 63
Llandolt iodine clock 41
luciferase 104
luminol 45, 50

M

malonic acid 45
Manual for Heads of Science 111
Maplin Electronics 60, 120
materials 66, 73
Mathematica 106
Mathematica in Education 106
Maxwell's theory 69
Mayan Indians 30
mercury 16–17
mercury lights 16, 17
metal coils 10
metal halide lights 17
metal rulers 14–15, 62–3
methane 24
methanol 24
methylated spirits 101
Microsoft Encarta 108
Miltrain Ltd 46, 104, 120–1
molecular modelling, web sites 110
monochromatic light 51–2

moon 22–3, 52
motivation 3
multimedia 105–6
Multimedia Toolbook 106
music 43
mutation, DNA 88–9

N

National Curriculum 66
National Radiological Protection Board 53
National Science Week 2
neon lasers *see* helium/neon lasers
neon lights 16, 18–19
NetNanny 107
Newton, Sir Isaac 7, 13
Newtonian liquids 72
Newton's Rings 30, 31
non-Newtonian liquids 72–9

O

optical fibres 56–7, 58–60
optics, web sites 108
oscillating reactions 43–5
osmosis 93–5
oxygen 40–1

P

parallax 25–7
participation 3, 4
particles, light scattering 29–30
periodic table, web sites 110
Philip Harris Scientific 9, 119–20
phosphors 17
phosphorus pentoxide 78
photographs, photosynthesis 92–3
photosynthesis 92–3
physics, web sites 107–8
plants
 capillary action 96–7
 indicators 89–91
plastics 34, 35
polarisation
 laser light 54–5
 light 32–8
Polaroid film 32–3, 34, 35, 36–7
Polaroid instant cameras 22
Polo mints 51
polybutadiene 68
poly(ethylene oxide) 73–5
polymeric sulphur 81
polymers 65–6
 size 66–8
 see also crystallisation; non-Newtonian liquids;

Index

polymeric sulphur; polyurethane foam; rubber
polyurethane foam 79–81
potassium bromate 45
Powerpoint 105
practice 5
presentation packages 105–6
primary colours 9
prisms 7–9, 12–13
projectors 8–9, 28–9
protective clothing 3, 5, 49

rod-climbing polymer solutions 75–6
Royal Institution 1, 41, 117
Royal Society 2, 115
Royal Society of Chemistry 116–17
RS Electronics Components Ltd 120
Rubber 68
    elasticity 68–70
    rubber bands 11, 71

Q

quartz-halogen lamps 18–19

R

Radiation Safety of Laser Products (BS) 54
Radio-Electronics 63
radios 10
rainbows 12–14
Reader, Phillip 116
redox reactions 40–1
refractive index 8
rheology 72
    see also elasticity; viscosity
robotic telescopes 25, 108

S

safety 3, 4, 5, 111
    lasers 55, 111–13
safety screens 5
Sam Houston University 49
sausage casings 95
scattering, polarisation 33–4
School Science Review 117
School Works 116
Schools Internet 107
Science Alive 116
Science Line 115
Science Museum 2
Science Projects 116
Scientific American 110
Scott-Bader Co Ltd 121
search engines 106–7

self-siphoning liquids 73–5
semiconductor lasers 112
Shakhashiri, B Z 43–5, 46, 49–50
Sigma Chemical Company Ltd 121
simplicity 4
single lens reflex (SLR) cameras 15, 21–2
slime 78–9
slinkies 10
soap 31
sodium hydrogen sulphite 43
sodium hydroxide 41, 48–9, 78
sodium lights 16, 18–19
software 105–6
sound 10–11
   and lasers 58–60, 63
   web sites 110
spectroscopy 20, 23–4
spectrum analysis charts 22
stars 23–5
street lights 22
stress birefringence 34–5
sucrose molecules 37
sucrose solution 35–7
sulphur 81
sulphur dioxide 43
sulphuric acid 45
sun 22, 23
sunglasses 33

suppliers
   chemicals 120–1
   lasers and optics 119–20
surface tension 98–100
Surfwatch 107
synthetic rubber 68

T

Talking Science+ 115
Taylor, C 45
telescopes, web sites 25, 108
televisions 9
TELOS/Springer-Verlag 106
temperature
   and elasticity 69–72
   light bulbs 16
   light sticks 46
   stars 23
thermo-elastic effect 69–72
total internal reflection (TIR) 55–60
triboluminescence 50–1
tripods 15, 23
troughs 10, 11–12
tungsten 16, 22
Tyndall effect 27–9
Tyndall, John 27

Index

U

ultraviolet light 17
Union Carbide Chemicals 121
universities 116–17
University of California 25, 108
University of Iowa 25, 108
US Activities Exchange 109

V

vinyl records 14–15
viscosity 66–8, 72, 74
visibility 4
visual authoring systems 106
visual impact 3
volcanoes, web sites 109

W

water
   and lasers 58
   oxygenation 40–1
   pH 39–40
   see also osmosis
water vapour 24
wave experiments 10–12
wave machines 12

wavelength
   laser light 60–3
   light 7–8
web sites 106–10
   astronomy and stars 25
   chemiluminescence 49
   Mathematica 106
   science questions 115
Wellcome Trust 115
wheat 85–8
white light 7–15, 51
Wolfram Research Inc 106

X

xenon lamps 19
xylophones 11

Y

Young's double slit experiment 60–2

Z

zinc sulphate crystals 50